Flowers
[**1001**]
[photos]

REBO PUBLISHERS

Contents

Beautiful Exotics

Wildflowers

Garden Flowers

Flowers of the Imagination

Flowers in Extreme Habitats

Beautiful Exotics

Tropical jungles are home to more than half the world's animal and plant species. In this universe, seasons do not exist and plants produce their flowers and fruit all year long.

With warm, constant temperatures and close to 100% humidity, a luxuriant and exuberant plant life grows at astonishing speed. The "masters" of this place are the trees. Like cathedrals of the plant world, they often grow to over 200 ft. (60 m) in height. Branching at a great height, they grow tightly packed together and, to keep themselves steady, the base of their trunk is reinforced with natural buttressing. It is on and around these trees that the life of the forest develops. In this shimmering universe, a ruthless battle is fought to conquer new territory and reach for the light. Their branches and even their leaves become home to a multitude of species that live on the decomposing particles that fall from the tree tops, creating vast suspended gardens. Some, like the lianas (woody vines), climb upwards, twisting themselves around the trunks in their quest for light; one of the most formidable of these is the strangler fig. Other species take advantage of these tall trees by sinking their root suckers down into them to draw off the nourishment they need. Exhausted by these parasites and stifled by lianas, the tree inexorably fades and dies. In tropical forests, trees die standing. Their death will eventually lead to that of their "guests" and

Flowers of the Jungle

also their "killers." But, before disappearing completely, decomposing under fungi, the trees will act as a host to "saprophytes"; plants which live on decaying plant matter. These plants prepare the ground for a new cycle of plant life. All the elements of this universe are closely interlinked. Tropical forests are extremely fragile biotopes and are increasingly endangered.

[1] *Drymonia rubra*, native to Costa Rica and Guatemala.
[2] Rangoon Creeper (*Quisqualis indica*), a climber from Burma with fragrant flowers.
[3] Crepe Ginger (*Costus speciosus*), native to India.
[4] *Brachychilum horsfieldii*, [5] *Dombeya x cayeuxii* and [6] Episcia (*Episcia splendens*), all native to Sri Lanka.

[1] *Alpinia zerumbet* and [2] Red Ginger (*Alpinia purpurata*), tropical plants that have become houseplants.
[3] Glory Lily (*Gloriosa rothschildiana*), a climber from Uganda with a poisonous bulb.
[4] Hibiscus 'Variegata' (*Hibiscus rosa-sinensis*), a plant from China with variegated leaves.
[5] *Greyia sutherlandii*, native to the Transvaal, in northern South Africa.

[Opposite] *Dombeya mastersii*.
[1] *Grevillea robusta*, native to Queensland, Australia; its flowers are pollinated by hummingbirds.
[2] Heliconia (*Heliconia rostrata*) and [3] Pink Ginger (*Alpinia purpurata* var. *rosea*), commonly cultivated in tropical gardens.

[1] Beehive Ginger (*Zingiber spectabile*), native to Malaysia.
[2] The Shellflower (*Alpinia speciosa*) is used as a medicinal plant in China.
[3] Golden Trumpet Vine (*Allamanda cathartica*), native to Brazil.
[4] *Ixora coccinea*, native to India.

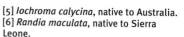

[5] *Iochroma calycina*, native to Australia.
[6] *Randia maculata*, native to Sierra Leone.
[7] Rafflesia (*Rafflesia* sp.), the world's largest flower, 47 in. (1.2 m) in diameter.
[8] *Calathea burlemarxii*, named for Burle Marx, the Brazilian landscape designer.

19

Orchids account for more than a tenth of the world's flowers, with more than 30,000 species. They can be found all over the planet but are most abundant in tropical forests.

Adorned with flowers of extraordinary beauty, form, color, and fragrance, orchids employ a vast range of behaviors in order to live, bloom, and multiply. The majority of tropical varieties are epiphytes – plants that grow on other plants rather than having their roots in the soil, and which find their nourishment by capturing the microorganisms contained in the rainwater that streams over them.

There was little understanding of this type of plant until the nineteenth century, when it came by sheer accident. One day, William Cattley, a keen enthusiast of exotic plants, received a shipment of tropical plants from Brazil. To protect them, they had been wrapped in thick leaves. Cattley

Tropical Orchids

potted up his new acquisitions and consigned the plant materials used for packaging to a corner of his greenhouse. Imagine his surprise a few weeks later to discover that magnificent flowers were emerging from these leaves. They were orchids. As a tribute to their accidental discoverer, they were named *Cattleya*. However, an unknown factor, and a very significant one, remained. How did orchids reproduce? All attempts at germination failed and not until 1909 did a Frenchman, Noël Bernard, demonstrate that in the wild, orchid seeds lived symbiotically with a fungus and that without its presence germination was impossible. In the 1960s, Georges Morel discovered that the growing tip of plants, known as the meristem, could be used to produce new plants by micropropagation. A small scrap of plant tissue from an orchid was sufficient to produce thousands of new, perfectly identical specimens.

[1] *Encyclia chimborazoensis*, native to Ecuador.
[2] *Cattleya labiata*, the first orchid to flower under glass.
[3] *Pleurothallis* sp., a genus containing more than 900 species.
[4] *Laelia cinnabarina*, native to Mexico.

[5] *Masdevallia* sp. A genus of more than 500 species.
[6] *Encyclia vespa*, native to Ecuador.
[7] *Epidendrum radicans*, native to Colombia.

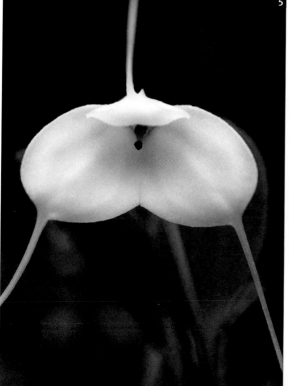

[1] *Cattleya harisoniana*, native to Costa Rica.
[2] *Masdevallia strobelii*, a high-altitude orchid.

[3] *Aspasia psitticina*, native to Brazil.
[4] *Masdevallia midas*, native to Ecuador.
[5] Bamboo Orchid (*Arundina graminifolia*), an orchid very commonly found in Caribbean gardens.
[6] *Epidendrum medusae*, native to Ecuador.

[far left] *Zygopetalum* sp. A genus of
Amazonian orchids that has been much
hybridized.
[1] *Epidendrum eburneum*, native to
Ecuador.
[2] *Elleanthus* sp. A genus of more than 100
species.
[3] *Cattleya maxima*, native to Ecuador.

[1] *Phragmipedium besseae*, an orchid discovered in Peru in 1981.
[2] *Cattleya* x 'Fukoo.' This genus has been hybridized with Laelias and *Brassias* to produce very large, fragrant orchids.
[3] *Masdevallia hirtzii*, native to Ecuador.

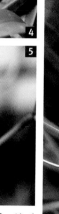

[4] *Masdevallia bonplandii* is named for Aimé Bonpland, who discovered it.
[5] *Oncidium macranthum*, native to Peru.
[6] *Pleurothallis* sp. The majority of orchids of this genus emit a foul aroma.

Some species that have no contact with the soil, live by trapping the humidity in the air and minute particles of plant waste carried by the rainwater that runs over them. Bromeliads are past masters at this form of survival.

Often known as "air plants," these species are able to store what they need to survive and develop despite having an extremely limited or totally non-existent root system. They do this directly through their leaves, which are covered in tiny hairs that trap food and humidity.

Air Plants

Perched high up in trees, they compensate for the lack of a growing medium by having leaves that are tightly interwoven in a spiral to create a central, watertight reservoir where rainwater and particles of decomposing plant material falling on to the host tree accumulate. This natural larder is home to an entire world that reproduces, lives, and dies, insects above all. The plant often produces flowers in the center of this bowl so that its pollen will be transported by the birds that come to devour these insects. The vast majority of these plants are pollinated by hummingbirds and, to attract them, they put out magnificently colored flowers. Every part of the plant has its own particular appeal. The leaves change color, becoming bright red, violet, yellow, or multi-colored. From these brightly colored leaf clusters, which are highly attractive to birds, small fragrant flowers emerge. Often ephemeral, they are followed by seeds which are also propagated by birds and therefore come in an array of bright colors. Once the reproductive cycle reaches an end, the leaves turn green again. Bromeliads often grow as close neighbors of epiphytic orchids in tropical forests, but can also be found in more arid areas.

[1] *Quesnelia* sp.
[2] and [7] *Puya* sp. This genus includes the largest bromeliads.
[3] *Neoregelia carolinae* and [6] *Neoregelia concentrica*. Their flower sits in a bowl of sugary liquid.
[4] *Tillandsia ionantha*. Once it comes into flower, the foliage turns red.
[5] *Oncidium kramerianum*. This orchid produces a solitary flower carried on a stem over 15 in. (40 cm) long.

[1] *Guzmania* sp. This genus from Brazil has been used to produce numerous houseplants.
[2] *Tillandsia* sp. This genus contains more than 500 species.
[3] Little Comet (*Angraecum eburneum*). An orchid that grows on tree trunks in Madagascar.
[far right] The magnificent red flowers of the orchid cactus (*Epiphyllum* sp.) attract hummingbirds.

[1] *Neoregelia inca.* The tiny flowers of this plant are very fragrant.
[2] *Dendrobium fimbriatum.* An orchid native to Burma and India.
[3] *Bilbergia* hybrid.

[4] *Bilbergia nutans*. Its pendant flowers are known as "Queen's Tears."
[5] *Nidularium innocentii*, native to Brazil.
[6] *Dendrobium aggregatum*, native to Burma and India.

[1] *Epidendrum ciliare* is one of the oldest known American orchids.
[2] *Vriesea psittacina.*
[3] *Tillandsia cyanea*, native to Ecuador and much cultivated as a houseplant.
[4] *Tillandsia cacticola*, a bromeliad found growing on cactuses.
[5] *Tillandsia* sp.
[6] *Aechmea fasciata*, the wild form of this bromeliad, which has become a very popular houseplant.

Flowers discovered that fragrance was an excellent way of attracting insects. And it is in tropical regions, where competition between species is tough, and in desert areas where pollinators are rare, where flowers unleash their most powerful perfumes.

The story of perfume essences dates back to the dawn of time. Perfumes appear in the legends of the gods and in the traditions of mankind. We burn aromatic woods; sandalwood and myrrh are burned in honor of Vishnu and Shiva. Egypt produced numerous learned writings on the art of perfumery; these provided a wealth of recipes used by enthusiasts of the time who drenched their bodies in perfumed oils and unguents such as myrtle, iris, jasmine, and rose. Rich Egyptian ladies were fond of wearing hollow earrings filled with perfume as well as necklaces containing sachets of aromatic seeds. The perfume trail that began in Egypt reached Rome and the city very soon became the

imperial capital of perfume, giving rise to the term *per fumum* ("through smoke"), from which the word "perfume" is derived. Later, in the Middle Ages, new species began to arrive from the Middle East such as lemon, orange, bergamot, and cistus. These new fragrant plants originating in the countries of the "infidels" were soon prohibited by the Roman Catholic Church, as indeed was mint, which was accused of "inciting marvelously to lust." With the coming of the Renaissance, the first apothecary shops began to offer the wealthiest members of society a range of preparations based on perfume essences and made to jealously guarded recipes. The seventeenth century saw the appearance of cologne. This was the period when the town of Grasse in southern France became the perfume capital

Bewitching Fragrances

of the world. French "noses" (or perfumers) are world renowned and their creations have made France the world center for luxury perfume. Guerlain created Shalimar, and Jean Patou created Joy, for many years considered to be the world's most expensive perfume. But first and foremost, it was Chanel and her famous Chanel Number 5 that conquered the world market. And it remains the most widely sold of all French perfumes.

[1] Ylang-ylang (*Cananga odorata*).
In Indonesia, its fragrance is claimed
to be an aphrodisiac.
[2] Queen of the Night (*Selenicereus
grandiflorus*). The highly fragrant flowers
of this plant only open for a few hours
at night.
[3] Orange tree (*Citrus sinensis*). Its
blossom emits a heady fragrance.
[4] Devil's Trumpet (*Datura metel*). The
fragrance of its flowers is similar to that
of some suntan oils.

[5] *Brugmansia sanguinea*. In the middle of the day its flowers give off a fruity fragrance.

[6] Blue Gum Eucalyptus (*Eucalyptus globulus*). The whole plant emits a powerful fragrance.

[7] Lemon Tree (*Citrus sinensis*). The smell of its blossom is reminiscent of its fruit.

[1] Wax Flower (*Hoya carnosa*). In the middle of the day, its flowers release highly fragrant droplets.

[2] Common Jasmine (*Jasminum officinale*). It is mainly in the evening that its flowers are at their most fragrant.

[3] Ylang-ylang (*Cananga odorata*) is one of the plants most used in perfumery.

[4] Shooting Stars (*Hoya multiflora*).

[right] Blue Gum Eucalyptus (*Eucalyptus globulus*). The pollen stored in its stamens is also strongly scented.

[1] Giant Himalayan Lily (*Cardiocrinum giganteum*). After two years, its giant bulb produces strongly scented flowers and then dies.
[2] *Brugmansia* x *insignis*.
[3] The Frangipani Tree (*Plumeria acutifolia*) is a common sight in tropical gardens and blooms all year round.
[4] Clary Sage (*Salvia sclarea*). This biennial produces lemon-scented flowers.

[5] Dragon Arum (*Arum dracunculus*). Only flies enjoy the foul smell of its giant flower.
[6] Wax Plant or Porcelain Flower (*Hoya carnosa* 'Picta').
[7] Gardenia (*Gardenia jasminoides*). Originating in China, the flower was worn as a boutonniere by the Romantics.

To ensure their union and fertilization, plants that are attached to the soil have to make use of "go-betweens." Wind, insects, birds, mammals, and even man often become the unintentional facilitators of their marriage.

Most species have chosen wind as their means of pollination. This method enables plants located several miles apart to "come together." Unfortunately, the pollen does not necessarily fall on to a specimen of the same species, and the wastage can be enormous. Other more sophisticated flowers have decided to form an alliance with animals to ensure their union. In exchange for food and other treats – sugary nectar, for example – these plants ensure that their pollen is transported on the backs and legs of certain creatures, and even in their stomach and excrement. Insects are the main facilitators of plant union. Often

Strange Unions

they are specialized, visiting only one species which is perfectly adapted to their morphology and way of life. Other creatures are also involved in the marriage of flowers; one Australian protea puts its flowers out horizontally along the ground so that they can be visited by a small mouse. Birds also make very effective partners, and plants produce strikingly colored flowers to attract them. Certain other species make use of bats. The so-called "cannonball tree" produces large, orange-red flowers sprouting directly from the trunk. The shape and arrangement of the petals are in exactly the same proportions as a satellite dish. This plant radar sends back a perfect echo of the signals the bats emit to guide themselves in the dark. The bats then land in the center of the flowers where they find fragrant nectar, and also pollen, which they then carry off to another flower. Once fertilized, the flowers will go on to produce large, rounded fruit more than 8 in. (20 cm) across that look like cannonballs.

[1] Marvel of Peru (*Mirabilis jalapa*). Its flowers only open and emit their fragrance at the end of the day.
[2] White Campion (*Lychnis vespertina*). The white color of its flowers attracts nocturnal insects.
[3] Morning Glory (*Convolvulus tricolor*). Its colorful flowers only open only in full sunlight.
[4] Friar's Cowl (*Arisarum vulgare*).
[5] Meadow Clary Sage (*Salvia pratensis*). Only large bumblebees manage to reach the nectar found at the base of the corolla.

[6] *Angraecum sesquipedale*. A sphinx moth with a 12 in. (30 cm) proboscis is the only moth able to collect the nectar found at the bottom of this orchid's spur.

[7] Carrion Plant (*Stapelia hirsuta*). The rotting smell and appearance of this plant make it attractive to flies.

[8] The Cuckoo Pint (*Arum maculatum*) emits a powerful scent that attracts aphids.

[9] Spring Gentian (*Gentiana verna*).

[1] *Paphiopedilum micranthum*, an orchid discovered in China in 1951.
[2] Cannonball Tree (*Couroupita guianensis*). Its dish-shaped flowers attract bats.

[3] *Paphiopedilum haynaldianum*, an orchid native to the Philippines.
[4] Scorpion Weed (*Phacelia tanacetifolia*), thought to be one of the most melliferous (honey-forming or bearing) plants.
[5] White Bird of Paradise (*Strelitzia alba*). Its flowers are fertilized by hummingbirds.

[1] Red Horsechestnut (*Aesculus* x *carnea*). Its flowers are not attractive to insects so the tree does not produce chestnuts.
[2] Gentian Sage (*Salvia patens*).
[3] *Huernia zebrina*.
[4] Purple Gentian (*Gentiana purpurea*). The flowers of this species always remain closed, so it is self-fertilizing.

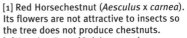

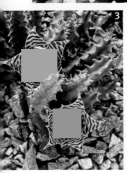

64

[5] *Catasetum pileatum* 'Imperiale.'
[6] *Lampranthus roseus.*
[7] Horse Chestnut (*Aesculus hippocastanum*). The small yellow mark in the center of the flower turns red when it has been fertilized.
[8] *Trichoceros antennifera.* The flower of this orchid resembles a fly.

65

Common Milkweed (*Asclepias cornutii*). Its flowers are equipped with claws that trap the legs of insects that come to visit it.

Flowers have developed an entire and often very aggressive arsenal of weapons to attract pollinators and to protect themselves. Traps, poisons, and irritant juices allow plants to survive and multiply.

Ceropegias prove formidable assailants when it comes to insects. At the top of their corollas are tiny hairs that move about in the wind. Aphids mistake these downy beds for a group of their fellow creatures. They hurry inside and down the length of the flower, attracted by an irresistible fragrance. Once they reach the bottom they discover that the smell was nothing but a lure. The insects then try to go back up, but unfortunately for them escape is impossible as the inner walls of the flower are covered in downward-pointing hairs. Imprisoned, they struggle to escape and become covered in pollen. It is not until the flower has faded that they are able to make their escape – if they have not already died of exhaustion.

The *Asclepias* (milkweed) is just as sadistic. No sooner do wasps come to collect nectar from it, landing on its stamens, than these close around them, trapping the insects' legs. Only the strongest manage to break free from the flower, though with its pollen stuck firmly to them. The others die on the spot.

With alocasias, it is snails that come under attack. Attracted by the strong odor of decay, the snails slide down the pollen-covered spathe. However, the powdery pollen very quickly becomes an irritant and they flee...only to enter another alocasia where, this time, it is a corrosive liquid that the flower releases on them. Twisting in pain, they struggle and in the process deposit –

Strange Behavior

albeit involuntarily – the pollen with which they became covered during their first visit.

In the evening, the flower of the *Victoria* becomes fragrant and attracts large cockchafers. At nightfall the flowers close, trapping their visitors inside. All day long the cockchafers struggle in vain to escape but it is not until the following day that the flower, now pink and odorless, releases them.

68

[[1] Mountain Avens (*Dryas octopetala*). Its flowers act like mini solar ovens and many aphids visit them to warm themselves up.
[2] Ivy-leaved Toadflax (*Linaria cymbalaria*). This plant, with its seeds carried on long peduncles, is self-seeding.
[3] Banana Passion Flower (*Passiflora mollissima*) and [7] Red Passionflower (*Passiflora manicata*).
[4] Madagascar Pitcher Plant (*Nepenthes madagascariensis*). A carnivorous plant from Madagascar.
[5] Ceropegia (*Ceropegia chrysantha*).
[6] Mossy Rockfoil (*Saxifraga muscoides*). This plant forms a ball to protect itself from the cold.

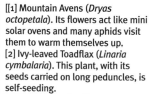

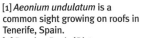

[1] *Aeonium undulatum* is a common sight growing on roofs in Tenerife, Spain.
[2] Burning Bush (*Dictamnus albus*). This plant gives off such a strong essence that it can burst into flame in the sun.
[3] Red Banana Passionflower (*Passiflora antioquiensis*).
[4] Greater Broomrape (*Orobanche rapum*). A parasitic plant.
[right] Scarlet Milkweed (*Asclepias curassavica*). Its flowers are fearsome insect traps.

[1] The Fetid Passionflower (*Passiflora foetida*) produces a poisonous fruit.
[2] Narrow-leaf Cotton Plant (*Gomphocarpus fruticosus*), also known as the "Tennis Ball Bush."
[3] Mexican Turk's Cap (*Malvaviscus arboreus*). Its flowers never open.

[4] The Madagascar Pitcher Plant (*Nepenthes madagascariensis*) traps insects as well as small amphibians.

[5] The Swan's Neck Agave (*Agave attenuata*) flowers only once, and then dies.

[6] Ivy-leaved Toadflax (*Linaria cymbalaria*) is also sometimes known as Rome's Ruin, because it destroys walls where it grows.

[7] Cytinus hypocistis (*Cytinus hypocistis*). A parasitic plant found in Corsican scrubland.

Giant Pelican Flower
(*Aristolochia gigantea*). The
name of this plant is derived
from "aristos" (excellent) and
"lokia" (giving birth) because it
has the reputation of making
pregnant women go into labor.

F rom the tiny flowers of the water lentil with only one stamen and a single ovary, to the giant rafflesia of Borneo, the flower world has experimented with every conceivable size, shape, and color.

Leafless and stemless, the rafflesia is only visible when it flowers. But when this happens it is impossible to miss: It produces a bright red corolla more than 3 ft. (1 m) in diameter that gives off a rank odor that can be smelled from a considerable way away. It is the world's largest flower and also the heaviest – weighing over 33 lb. (15 kg). Other lighter and more discreet species make up for the lack of attraction provided by their small flowers by grouping them together in clusters and surrounding them with transformed leaves. In this way, the whole inflorescence mimics perfectly a single, large, "true" flower. The composite family has used this method to produce daisies, sunflowers, and edelweiss. Other species ensure that a number

of their leaves are colored, giving them the appearance of petals; this is true of bougainvilleas, some euphorbias, and a strange plant found in tropical forests. *Cephaelis tomentosa* has two terminal leaves surrounding the flowers which look exactly like a pair of fleshy lips. Every color of the rainbow is represented, although green and black remain extremely rare. Species that are wind pollinated do not depend on being visited by insects and

Strange Forms

often prefer to produce green flowers which can be perfectly concealed among their foliage. As for black, only two species can genuinely be said to be this color. The most beautiful is a fritillary that grows in Siberia; the other is a gentian known as the "flor de muerto" (dead man's flower). Other plants that are said to be black are in fact only dark purple, as is the case with tulips.

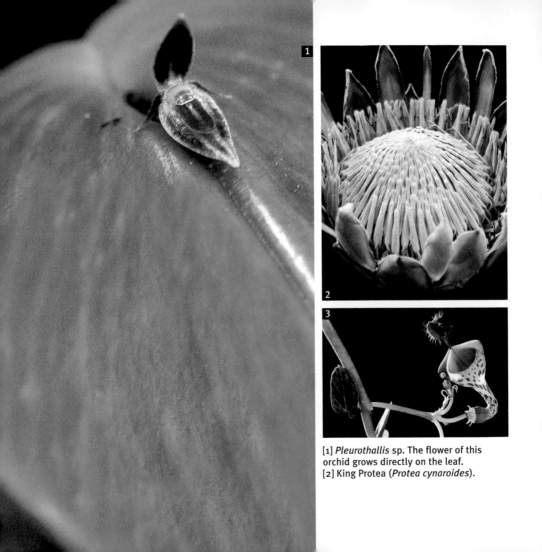

[1] *Pleurothallis* sp. The flower of this orchid grows directly on the leaf.
[2] King Protea (*Protea cynaroides*).

[3] This Ceropegia (*Ceropegia distincta*) and [4] Parachute Plant (*Ceropegia sandersonii*) are native to South Africa. [5] The Lizard Orchid (*Himantoglossum hircinum*) has a long labellum. [6] The Bird of Paradise (*Strelitzia reginae*) is so called because its flowers are fertilized by hummingbirds.

79

[1] *Mussaenda luteola*. In Africa, the roots of this plant are believed to cure snake bites.
[2] and [5] Poinsettias (*Euphorbia pulcherrima*) are native to Mexico.
[3] *Calathea crotalifera*. Its flowers resemble a rattlesnake.
[4] *Dracula chimaera*, an orchid from Ecuador.

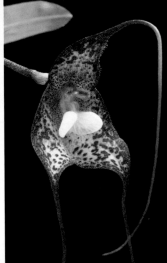

[6] Woodrose (*Ipomoea tuberosa*). As the flowers fade, the petals become brown and hard, hence its common name.

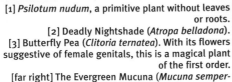

[1] *Psilotum nudum*, a primitive plant without leaves or roots.
[2] Deadly Nightshade (*Atropa belladona*).
[3] Butterfly Pea (*Clitoria ternatea*). With its flowers suggestive of female genitals, this is a magical plant of the first order.
[far right] The Evergreen Mucuna (*Mucuna sempervirens*) has foul-smelling flowers.

[1] Swiss Cheese Plant (*Monstera deliciosa*). The edible fruit of this plant tastes of banana and pineapple.
[2] *Hasclobergui grasneri* has fluorescent green flowers.
[3] The magical bulb of the Voodoo Lily (*Sauromatum venosum*) blooms without water or soil.

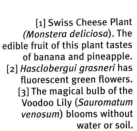

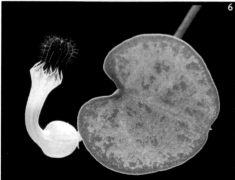

[4] *Cephaelis tomentosa*. The strange flowers of this plant have earned it the nickname "Fiancée's Kiss" in French.
[5] This Ceropegia (*Ceropegia woodii*) has heart-shaped leaves.
[6] Viola cornuta 'Molly Sanderson' produces one of the plant world's blackest flowers.

Spice-producing and strongly flavored plants are mainly found in the warm regions of the world. The history of the great civilizations, their development, and their power are closely linked to the conquest of these plants.

It was via Rome that the western world became acquainted with spices. Later, with the crusades, men who had grown up in cold climates were introduced to the warm and bewitching charms of spices. Up to the end of the fifteenth century, the spice trade was the exclusive domain of the city of Venice, which was supplied directly by Arab merchants. To break this monopoly, Portugal embarked on an unprecedented scientific and technological campaign. Three ships were fitted out and placed under the command of Vasco da Gama. The fleet set sail from the port of Lisbon on July 8, 1497. Da Gama rounded the Cape of Good Hope, went back up the coast of Africa and crossed the Indian Ocean. He eventually reached Cochin in south-west India. This was indeed spice paradise, with pepper, cinnamon, ginger, and turmeric all readily available. Spain, with Christopher Columbus, decided to get to India via a western route. On August 3, 1492, three ships set sail from the port of Palos. On October 12th, they sighted land. Columbus expressed his surprise at reaching India so quickly, but it was, of course, America. On this new continent, Columbus discovered vanilla and peppers. The Dutch also decided to go off in pursuit of spices. They conquered the Moluccan Islands and became the sole exporters of nutmeg and cloves. As for the

Fiery Flavors

French, they had to wait for the talents of the aptly named Auguste Poivre ("poivre" is pepper in French!). Taking advantage of the disputes raging between the Spanish, English, and Portuguese, French pirates under Poivre's command succeeded in stealing some nutmeg and clove trees, which were planted in the famous Jardin des Pamplemousses on the island of Mauritius.

[1-4-5] The flowers of the Vanilla Orchid (*Vanilla fragrans*) are fertilized by hand. They produce an odorless pod which only releases its aroma after it has been fermented and dried.
[2] Wild Mustard (*Sinapis arvensis*).
[3] Nutmeg (*Myristica fragrans*).
[6] Black Pepper (*Piper nigrum*).

[1] Brazilian Pepper (*Schinus terebenthi-folius*). This tree produces pink pepper.
[2] Coriander (*Coriandrum sativum*). Used fresh in Africa and dried in Europe.
[3] The Saffron Crocus (*Crocus sativus*) is the source of the world's most expensive spice.

[4] Rue (*Ruta graveolens*) is highly valued in northern Africa.
[5] Black Pepper Tree (*Piper nigrum*). The seeds grow in clusters.
[6] Cinnamon Tree (*Cinnamomum zeylanicum*). The bark is the source of the famous Ceylon cinnamon.

[left] The Vanilla Orchid (*Vanilla fragrans*) is a climber with thick leaves and can grow to over 65 ft. (20 m) in length. [1] The Cinnamon Tree (*Cinnamomum zeylanicum*) is an evergreen member of the laurel family. [2] Black Pepper Tree (*Piper nigrum*). Pepper harvesting in India. [3] Fresh pods of vanilla (*Vanilla fragrans*).

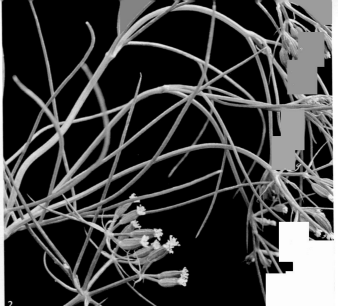

[1] Vanilla (*Vanilla fragrans*).
A plantation on Réunion Island.
[2] Cumin (*Cuminum cyminum*),
an annual native to central Asia
and Turkestan.
[3] Paprika (*Capsicum annuum*),
a sweet pepper grown in Hungary.
[4] Love-in-a-Mist (*Nigella damascena*).
[5] Turmeric (*Curcuma longa*).

99

Wildflowers

Unlike tropical orchids, European orchids plunge their roots into the soil. Though more modest, they are no less sophisticated in their form, color, and means of reproduction.

Europe boasts several hundred species and varieties of orchid. Although some of them, such as the Lady's Slipper orchid, remain rare and are in fact strictly protected, the majority are quite common. Their habitat is very varied: They are found growing under trees in woodland, in the mountains, on the coast, in meadows, on embankments, and even on the edge of pavements.

What makes orchids different from other European flowers is their relationship with insects. To attract pollinators, many plants have evolved appealing fragrances and sugary nectar. European orchids have added "sexual attraction" to this armory by inventing plant mimicry. The form of their flowers bears a curious resemblance to females of particular insect species. Attracted by this lure, the male insect lands on the orchid and desperately tries to mate with it. In his amorous struggles, he becomes covered with pollen and in a state of pique flies off to find another impostor female on which he will deposit this precious pollen, thus fertilizing the new plant. This strategy has become highly developed, as each species of orchid

European Orchids

mimics and attracts a single species of insect. The flower even manages to bloom just a few days before the real female insects become fertile and emits a fragrance, imperceptible to humans, but very similar to the pheromones released by the females during the mating period. Moreover, the hairs covering the petals are arranged in such a way that they are a perfect match for those found on the bodies of the female insects.

[1] Narrow-leaved Helleborine (*Cephalanthera longifolia*). Its flowers never open fully.

[2] Lady's Slipper Orchid (*Cypripedium calceolus*), the largest of the French orchids.

[3] The Giant Orchid (*Barlia robertiana*) and [6] Yellow Ophrys (*Ophrys lutea*) are orchids found in the Mediterranean region.

[4] Pyramidal Orchid (Anacamptis pyramidalis), one of the last to flower.

[5] Woodcock Orchid (*Ophrys scolopax*).

4

5

6

[far left] Red Vanilla Orchid (*Nigritella rubra*), so called because its flowers have a vanilla fragrance.
[1] Spider Orchid (*Ophrys sphegodes litigiosa*).
[2] Elder-flowered Orchid (*Dactylorhiza sambucina*).
[3] Man Orchid (*Aceras anthropophorum*).

[1] Lady Orchid (*Orchis purpurea*).
[2] Lesser Butterfly Orchid (*Platanthera bifolia*).
[3] Burnt Orchid (*Orchis ustulata*).
[4] Spider Orchid (*Ophrys sphegodes* ssp. litigiosa).
[5] Fly Orchid (*Ophrys muscifera*).
[6] Bee Orchid (*Ophrys apifera*).
[7] Monkey Orchid (*Orchis simia*).

[1] Heart-flowered Serapias (*Serapias cordigera*).
[2] Early Purple Orchid (*Orchis masculata*). The bulbs are boiled and mixed with honey to produce "salep," an aphrodisiac drink.
[far right] Green-winged Orchid (*Orchis morio*).

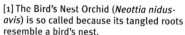

[1] The Bird's Nest Orchid (*Neottia nidus-avis*) is so called because its tangled roots resemble a bird's nest.
[2] Red Helleborine (*Cephalanthera rubra*).
[3] Giant Orchid (*Barlia robertiana*).
[4] Common Twayblade (*Listera ovata*).
[5] Lizard Orchid (*Himantoglossum-hircinum*). The flowers smell unpleasantly of goats.

Medicinal Plants

The medicinal use of plants is as old as mankind but it was only through countless trial and error experiments that we were able to identify the species useful to our health. The vast majority of molecules used today in medicinal substances are derived from plants.

The simple gathering of medicinal plants was soon replaced by early forms of cultivation. In ancient Egypt there were gardens devoted to medicinal plants. And simple absorption was soon replaced with skillful and often very complex preparations. In China, two thousand eight hundred years before the modern era, the "Yellow Emperor" wrote the first book of medicine and plant-based recipes. The Greeks and Romans, with Hippocrates, Theophrastus, Cato, and most importantly Celsus, raised the use of medicinal plants to the ranks of science. In the Middle Ages, it was in the monasteries that the therapeutic use of plants blossomed. Medicinal plants (known as "simples") were grown, and potions, liquors, and other elixirs were prepared. In the early fifteenth century, a physician known as Paracelsus established the "Doctrine of Signatures." He believed that all medicinal plants had a divine signature which ascribed to them a therapeutic purpose and particular properties.

However, during the period of the Enlightenment there was a move away from plant-based medicinal practice. It was not until the twentieth century that scientists once again became interested in traditional medicines. They confirmed many of the properties traditionally attributed to plants. One example is that of the willow. This tree, which often grows with its feet in water, was reputed to cure colds and chills as well as rheumatism and stiff joints, as its stems are soft and flexible. In fact, the medicinal substance isolated from its bark is acetylsalicylic acid, otherwise known as aspirin.

[1] Common Sage (*Salvia officinalis*). According to an old saying, "he who grows sage in his garden cannot die."
[2] Garden of medicinal plants.
[3] Quinine Tree (*Cinchona officinalis*). Its bark yields quinine.

[4] Yarrow (*Achillea millefolium*). Used in the past in exorcisms.
[5] St. John's Wort (*Hypericum perforatum*). When steeped in oil, the flowers can help to soothe burns.
[6] Motherwort (*Leonurus cardiaca*) calms palpitations.

[1] Greater Celandine (*Chelidonium majus*). The juice of its stems removes warts.
[2] White Deadnettle (*Lamium alba*). Used in many beauty products.
[3] Roman Chamomile (*Anthemis nobilis*) is a double-flowered variety used in herbal medicine.
[right] Common Mallow (*Malva sylvestris*). This is a soothing plant; its flowers are one of the species used in the "four-flower herbal infusion."

[1] Great Mullein (*Verbascum thapsus*). Its flowers soothe coughs.
[2] Herb Robert (*Geranium robertianum*).
[3] Lungwort (*Pulmonaria officinalis*). When dried, this plant is used to treat diarrhea, spitting of blood, and hemorrhoids.
[4] Ground Ivy (*Glechoma hederacea*).
[5] Marsh Mallow (*Althaea officinalis*). When chewed, the root can help to soothe the pain of inflamed gums.

[left] Golden Shower Tree (*Cassia fistula*). Cassia pods are used medicinally.
[1] Garlic Mustard (*Alllaria officinalis*) is a stimulant and diuretic.
[2] Pot Marigold (*Calendula officinalis*) is very effective in the treatment of biliary secretions.
[3] Lady's Mantle (*Alchemilla mollis*). In the early morning, the outer rim and center of its leaves are sprinkled with sparkling droplets of dew.
[4] *Aloe vera* is widely used in beauty products.

125

[1] Ground Ivy (*Glechoma hederacea*). This was once used in poultices to treat attacks of gout.
[2] Sweet Flag (*Acorus calamus*). The rhizome of this plant is used to flavor liqueurs and beer.

[3] Dandelion (*Taraxacum dens-leonis*)
is a powerful diuretic, hence its
old English name "piss-a-bed."
[4] Fenugreek (*Trigonella
foenum-graecum*).
[5] Pride of the Meadow (*Spiraea ulmaria*)
is a species in which acetylsalicylic acid
(aspirin) has been isolated.

127

Poisonous Plants

The flowers we find growing around us often contain fearsome poisons. And they can be all the more dangerous when they appear inoffensive. Every year, thousands of people fall victim to plant poisoning to varying degrees.

Among the plants that grow wild in our fields and meadows, the family Solanaceae contains some of the most highly poisonous species, such as deadly nightshade and henbane. (It is important not to confuse the formidable giant hemlock with chervil and parsley.) They are very common and can be extremely poisonous, containing five alkaloids, including conicine. Two drops on a dog's tongue are enough to kill it in three minutes. In humans, the resulting symptoms are rapid and death occurs with six hours of ingestion of certain parts of the plant. Similar in appearance to giant hemlock, the hemlock water dropwort was long used to make the infamous "celery broth." Efficiently administered, it could accelerate the death of relatives who were slow to die and thus help to solve inheritance problems. A piece of the root of this plant kills in less than two hours. However, the most poisonous members of European flora grow at high altitudes. These are the aconites: the blue-flowered common monkshood and the yellow-flowered wolfsbane. All parts of these plants, but mainly their roots, contain aconitine. Fatal doses vary between 1/5 oz. (5 g) of root in high altitude species and 3/5 oz. (15 g) in the lowland species. Romeo, Juliet's lover, poisons himself with aconite. In the Middle Ages, foxes and wolves were killed by putting out bait poisoned with aconite juice – hence the common name wolfsbane and the scientific name *Vulparia* (from the Latin vulpes: fox). It is possible for certain parts of plants to be poisonous while the remainder is edible.

[1] Wolfsbane (*Aconitum lycoctonum*) is one of the most poisonous plants.
[2] Lenten Rose (*Helleborus orientalis*). Contact with this plant can cause dermatitis.

[3] Laburnum (*Laburnum anagyroides*). Its seeds are deadly if ingested.
[4] Rhododendron (*Rhododendron*). The pollen of rhododendron flowers is poisonous to bees.
[5] The Pasqueflower (*Pulsatilla vulgaris*) is poisonous, as are all anemones.

[1] *Primula grandiflora.*
[2] The Common Foxglove (*Digitalis purpurea*) is poisonous but is also the source of some of the best drugs used to treat heart conditions.
[3] Deadly Nightshade (*Atropa belladona*). Two or three berries are enough to cause death.
[4] Staghorn Sumac (*Rhus typhina*). Its flower pollen is highly irritant.
[5] Trailing Nightshade (*Solanum dulcamara*). Though sweet to the taste, its fruits rapidly become irritant.
[6] Black Henbane (*Hyoscyamus niger*). According to Shakespeare, Hamlet's father was poisoned by having henbane juice poured into his ear while he was sleeping.

135

[left] Lenten Rose (*Helleborus orientalis*).
[1] Castor Bean Plant (*Ricinus communis*). Castor (or ricin) oil is obtained from its seeds.
[2] Poison Hemlock (*Conium maculatum*). This was the plant used to execute Socrates.
[3] Lily of the Valley (*Convallaria majalis*). Drinking a glass of water in which some sprigs of lily of the valley have been soaking is sufficient to cause death.

[1] Cuckoo Pint (*Arum maculatum*). Its red fruits cause severe inflammation of the mouth.
[2] Hemlock Water Dropwort (*Oenanthe crocata*). A piece of the root the size of a hazelnut is sufficient to kill a person within two hours.

[3] European Privet (*Ligustrum vulgare*), poisonous when fresh.
[4] Monkshood (*Aconitum napellus*). Just 1/8 oz. (4 g) of fresh root are enough to kill a person.
[5] White Bryony (*Bryonia dioica*).
[6] Rose Bay (*Nerium oleander*). Highly poisonous, 3 oz. (100 g) of rose bay leaf are enough to kill an ox.

Thousands of plants contain pigments used both in the manufacture of dyes and for dyeing fabrics, as well as to enhance or alter the color of certain foods. Every possible shade of color can be obtained from plants.

In the past, woad was used to dye fabric blue in Europe. The leaves were picked all year round and in the south of France made into a paste known as "cocagne," which colored wool a wonderful blue and was very durable. Madder root gave what was known as "vraie couleur" (true color) and Lower Normandy produced "écarlate de Caen" (Caen red), which was famous throughout Europe.

Yellow is the easiest color to obtain from plants. In France, the roots, leaves, and seeds of weld were used to produce luteoline, a dye considered to give the purest, finest yellow. Other plants used include goldenrod, dyer's broom, lichens, apple tree bark, and onion peel. Saffron also gives a wonderful yellow, but unfortunately the color is short-lived and excessively expensive to produce.

By mixing the three primary colors (blue, red, and yellow), it is possible to obtain every shade in the color spectrum. An almost black dye is extracted from the roots of certain plants, such as the yellow flag,

Dyer's Plants

which gives "body" to other dyes. Dipping a fabric first in weld and then in indigo produces a magnificent green. Madder followed by weld gives orange. Indigo added to madder produces violet. Madder, indigo, and weld together give a deep black. Colors can also be altered by "seasoning" dye baths with lemon juice, chalk, or alum.

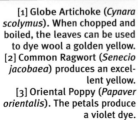

[1] Globe Artichoke (*Cynara scolymus*). When chopped and boiled, the leaves can be used to dye wool a golden yellow.
[2] Common Ragwort (*Senecio jacobaea*) produces an excellent yellow.
[3] Oriental Poppy (*Papaver orientalis*). The petals produce a violet dye.

[4] Purple Loosestrife (*Lythrum salicaria*). The flowers can be used as a red confectionery dye.
[5] Broom (*Sarothamnus scoparius*). The flowers give a green dye.

143

[left] Red Clover (*Trifolium pratense*).
All parts of the plant are used
as a lemon yellow dyestuff.
Before Himalayan Indigo (*Indigofera gerardiana*) [3] was available,
blue dyestuff was obtained from
Woad (*Isatis tinctoria*) [1].
[2] Hollyhock (*Alcea rosea*).
The flowers yield a blue dye.

147

[1] Wild Teasel (*Dipsacus silvestris*). This plant produces a very ephemeral blue dye.
[2] Strawberry Tree (*Arbutus unedo*). The bark gives a grayish brown dye.
[3] St. John's Wort (*Hypericum perforatum*). The flowers give red and green dye.
[4] Canada Goldenrod (*Solidago canadensis*). The flowers produce a bright yellow.
[5] Locust Tree (*Robinia pseudoacacia*). The wood of this tree gives a yellow dye.
[6] Golden Tickseed (*Coreopsis tinctoria*). The flowers give an orange dye.
[7] Yellowwort (*Chlora perfoliata*). When used with alum, this plant gives a yellow dye and with iron sulfate gives brown.

[1] Common Ragwort (*Senecio jacobaea*).
[2] Orange Cosmos (*Cosmos sulphureus*).
The flowers produce an orange dye.
[3] Hemp Agrimony (*Eupatorium cannabinum*). All parts of the plant give a yellow dye.
[4] Myrtle-leaved Coriaria (*Coriaria myrtifolia*). The bark gives a black dye.

[5] Bird Cherry (*Prunus padus*). The bark gives a violet dye.
[6] Dyer's Broom (*Genista tinctoria*). The flowers produce a yellow dye.
[7] White Mignonette (*Reseda alba*). The flowers give a yellow dye.

There are a large number of substances known as resins, balsams, gums, latex, mastic, and manna, all of which have one thing in common: They exist as fluids in plant tissue but thicken and harden on contact with the air.

As they solidify, resins become translucent, fragrant, and bitter-tasting. They are soluble in alcohol and ether, but insoluble in water. The two most famous resins are incense and amber, the latter being fossilized conifer resin. This type of amber, from which jewelry is made, is not to be confused with ambergris, which is produced by sperm whales and used in perfumery.

Balsams are very similar to resins. What differentiates them is the presence of benzoic or cinnamic acid, which gives them a very characteristic balsamic smell when heated. Balsams are insoluble in water but soluble in alcohol. The most famous are benzoin, styrax, balsam of Peru, balsam of Tolu and balsam of Mecca. All are obtained by "tapping" exotic trees. Styrax is extracted from the styrax tree (*Styrax officinale*), which produces two types of styrax: calamite which is solid, reddish brown, and shiny with a vanilla odor; and liquid styrax which is opaque and gray and used in perfumery.

The gums come mainly from trees of the family Leguminosae. They are transparent,

Plants Producing Sap, Resin, and Latex

do not crystallize, are odorless, and, most importantly, are insoluble in alcohol. They do, however, dissolve in water. The best known is gum arabic. Gum is spontaneously exuded from the bark of various trees found in Senegal and Egypt and from a number of acacias. Unlike resins, gums have a mild smell and taste.

[1] Fig Tree (*Ficus carica*). The white latex that seeps from the stems dissolves warts and corns.
[2] Hogweed (*Heracleum spondylium*). The sap from its stems is a strong irritant.
[3] The Mastic Tree (*Pistacia lentiscus*) produces a highly aromatic resin.
[4] Rock Rose (*Cistus albidus*). The leaves give off a fragrant substance.

[5] Cypress Spurge (*Euphorbia cyparissias*). The stems contain a poisonous latex.
[6] Bloodroot (*Sanguinaria canadensis*). The sap is blood red.

154

155

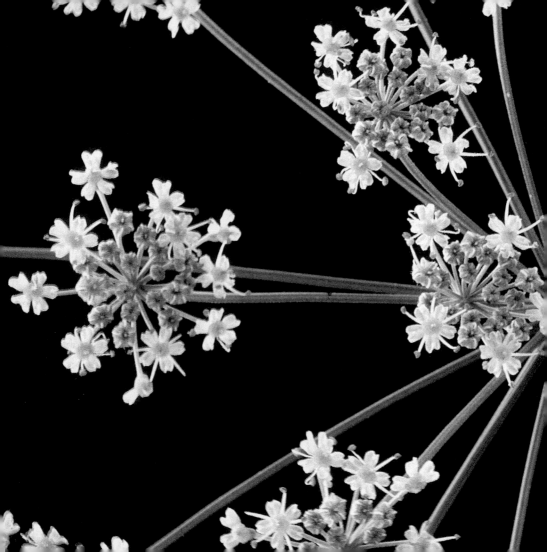

[1] The Characias Spurge (*Euphorbia characias*) has poisonous latex.
[2] Blue Gum Tree (*Eucalyptus globulus*). The leaves contain a very fragrant gum.
[3] Turpentine Tree (*Pistacia terebinthus*). Turpentine is obtained from its bark.
[4] Oriental Poppy (*Papaver orientalis*). Its milky sap is poisonous.

[5] Manna Ash (*Fraxinus ornus*). The leaves of this plant exude droplets that are said to be the "manna from heaven" referred to in the Bible.
[6] The California Poppy (*Eschscholzia californica*) contains a colorless latex.
[7] Sageleaf Rock Rose (*Cistus salvifolius*). The branches contain an ambergris-fragranced resin.

159

[1] Turpentine Tree (*Pistacia terebinthus*).
[2] Common Sow Thistle (*Sonchus oleraceus*) and [3] Prickly Sow Thistle
(*Sonchus asper*). The stems of these plants contain a milky sap.
[far right] Gum Rock Rose (*Cistus ladanifer*). The resin gives a blackish substance known as "laudanum."

[1] Wall Lettuce (*Mycelis muralis*). The stems contain a milky sap.
[2] and [6] Common Ash (*Fraxinus excelsior*).
[3] Greater Celandine (*Chelidonium majus*). Its yellow sap gets rid of warts.
[4] Blue Lettuce (*Lactuca perennis*). The stems contain a milky sap.
[5] Purple Rock Rose (*Cistus purpureus*). It has a very fragrant resin.

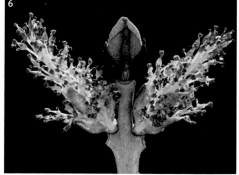

While the tropics and deserts are the home of spices, temperate zones are home to aromatic plants. Many are native to southern Europe but the colder regions also produce strongly flavored species. Also, certain exotics have become acclimatized to growing in our part of the world.

The umbellifer family is one of the richest providers of aromatic plants, including anise, chervil, parsley, dill, and fennel. It is often difficult to identify these species and this can cause problems as the family also includes some very dangerous members such as hemlock water dropwort, hogweed, and, most importantly, poison hemlock.

Another family that produces many aromatic plants is the labiates. Thyme, balm, wild thyme, the mints, and rosemary are all labiates. Most aromatic plants prefer growing in warmer regions and both their fragrance and taste are more pronounced when they grow in full sunshine. There are exceptions, however; calamints, sweet cicely, and lovage fare better at higher altitudes and in cool spots. Basil, rue, and lemon-scented verbena, which originate in Asia and Africa, are regularly cultivated in Mediterranean regions or grown as annuals. A large number of varieties have been created from the wild forms of these plants. Mints are available in a variety of different flavors. Thymes are also differently scented. New species have also

Aromatic Plants

appeared in the "aromatic plants" section of garden centers. They include monardas, which are native to North America and have a spicy flavor; *Mertensia maritima*, known as the "oyster plant," the leaves of which are edible and taste similar to oyster flesh; and Stevia rebaudiana, commonly known as the "sweetleaf" or "sugar leaf" because its leaves can be used as a sugar substitute.

[1] Chives (*Allium schoenoprasum*), a hardy plant with lilac-colored flowers.
[2] Chervil (*Anthriscus cerefolium*) is an annual.
[3] Sweet Cicely (*Myrrhis odorata*), a hardy plant with an aniseed smell.
[4] Common Valerian (*Valeriana officinalis*). Its aromatic root is attractive to cats.
[5] Creeping Thyme (*Thymus serpyllum*) is often found growing among rocks.
[6] Summer Savory (*Satureja hortensis*) is an annual.
[7] Rhubarb (*Rheum rhaponticum*). Only the stems are used, as the other parts of the plant are poisonous.

[1] Hyssop (*Hyssopus officinalis*). This plant is more strongly aromatic before it flowers.
[2] The Oyster Plant (*Mertensia maritima*) is so called because its leaves taste like oysters.
[3] Common Thyme (*Thymus vulgaris*) is frequently found growing on Mediterranean scrubland.
[4] Rosemary (*Rosmarinus officinalis*) flowers in late winter in mild areas.
[5] Rocket (*Eruca sativa*) is reputed to have aphrodisiac qualities.
[6] Oregano (*Origanum vulgare*) is widely used as a pizza flavoring.

[left] Caraway (*Carum carvi*). Its seeds are used to flavor sauerkraut.
[1] Pennyroyal (*Mentha pulegium*). Its smell drives away fleas.
[2] Fennel (*Foeniculum vulgare*). Its seeds are used to flavor fish dishes.
[3] Anise (*Pimpinella anisum*). The liqueur "pastis" is flavored with its seeds.

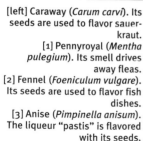

175

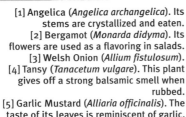

[1] Angelica (*Angelica archangelica*). Its stems are crystallized and eaten.
[2] Bergamot (*Monarda didyma*). Its flowers are used as a flavoring in salads.
[3] Welsh Onion (*Allium fistulosum*).
[4] Tansy (*Tanacetum vulgare*). This plant gives off a strong balsamic smell when rubbed.
[5] Garlic Mustard (*Alliaria officinalis*). The taste of its leaves is reminiscent of garlic.
[6] Basil (*Ocimum basilicum*) is a pot-grown annual.

4

5

6

I n nature, some species mimic their neighbors in order to protect or conceal themselves. Many plants have their doubles: false versions of various kinds that have been used honestly and dishonestly as substitutes for the real thing.

The leaves of white dead nettle do not sting, so they often conceal themselves by growing among other nettles as protection from attack by herbivores. The leaves are identical in form and it is only when the plant flowers that the two species can be told apart. People have been known to take advantage of this plant mimicry to substitute one product for another. For example, saffron, the most expensive of all the spices, is replaced by marigold or safflower pollen or by powdered turmeric root. The helichrysum known as the curry plant is used to produce a false version of curry powder. Nasturtium and hellebore seeds make excellent caper substi-

Impostor Plants

tutes. The blessed thistle is used in place of hops in low-quality beers. Coffee is impossible to grow in cool climates, but imitation versions have often been made by roasting the seeds of various wild plants including juniper, sweet chestnut, beech, oak, cotton, carob, astragalus, lupin, wild carrot, burdock, and, in particular, chicory and barley. Flour has been made from water lily seeds soaked in water to make them swell. It has also been made from birch sawdust and the under layer of willow bark. Parsnip roots have been used in place of sugar. Wood sorrel leaves taste very like vinegar. The roots of caper plants and coltsfoot ash can be used to produce a powder very similar to salt. Pepper also has

its doubles: nigella and chaste tree seeds. Scents too have their substitute versions – the rose essence obtained from rose petals is often replaced by the essence of a particular geranium, *Pelargonium rosea*, a close relative of the plants that adorn our balconies and window boxes in summer. The geranium family appears to be particularly adept at "odor mimicry."

[1] Chaste Tree (*Vitex agnus-castus*). Its seeds were often used instead of pepper.
[2] and [3] Greater Burdock (*Arctium lappa*). When roasted, its seeds can be used in place of coffee.
[4] and [8] Rose-scented Pelargonium (*Pelargonium graveolens*). Rose essence is extracted from its leaves.

[5] Scented-leaf Pelargonium 'Clorinda'
(*Pelargonium hybrid*). Its leaves smell
of pine.
[6] Creeping Woodsorrel (*Oxalis corniculata*)
is a four-leaved, false clover.
[7] Carob Tree (*Ceratonia siliqua*). The ripe
fruits have a chocolatey taste.

[1] Soapwort (*Saponaria officinalis*). This plant produces a soapy foam in water.
[2] Pineapple Sage (*Salvia rutilans*). When rubbed, its leaves smell of pineapple.
[3] Love-in-a-Mist (*Nigella damascena*). In Europe, its seeds were used in place of pepper.
[4] Pelargonium 'Paton's Unique' (*Pelargonium x fragrans*). Its leaves smell of apricot.
[5] Chicory (*Cichorium intybus*). When roasted, its root is used as a coffee substitute.

[left] Pelargonium 'Concolour Lace' (*Pelargonium hybrid*). Its leaves smell of hazelnut.
[1] Safflower (*Carthamus tinctorius*). Its flowers are often used instead of saffron.
[2] Pelargonium 'Prince of Orange' (*Pelargonium hybrid*). Its leaves smell of oranges.
[3] Scented-leaf Pelargonium (*Pelargonium x fragrans*). Its leaves smell of pine.
[4] Caper Spurge (*Euphorbia lathyris*). Its fruit are used as counterfeit capers.

[1] Chilean Wood Sorrel (*Oxalis adenophylla*) is a four-leaved false clover.
[2] Pelargonium 'Scarlet Unique' (*Pelargonium hybrid*). Its leaves smell of carrot tops.
[3] Coltsfoot (*Tussilago farfara*). Its leaves are used as a tobacco substitute.
[4] Lupin (*Lupinus* x *polyphyllus*). Its seeds are used as a coffee substitute.
[5] Euphorbia (*Euphorbia* sp.). When soaked in vinegar, the fruits of this plant can be used as a substitute for capers.

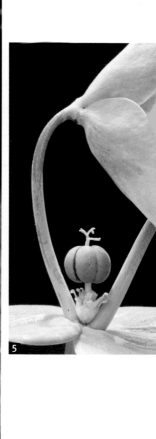

4

5

189

Garden Flowers

A garden without roses is not a garden. Since antiquity, the 100 or so wild species of rose, all of them native to the northern hemisphere, have been crossed to produce thousands of varieties of different sizes, fragrances, and colors, with the exception of blue.

The first roses appeared 35 million years ago, probably in Siberia, and are believed to have found their way to China and America over the Bering Strait. The ancestor of all roses is *Rosa beggeriana*. Its white flowers smell of hazelnut. This species still grows in the province of Xinjiang in China. And it was in China that the majority of wild roses originated, some of which are still found in Europe, and in France in particular with the pimpernel rose in the Alps and the seraphim rose in Corsica. Wild roses crossed in nature to produce the first natural hybrids and these in turn crossed with other roses. And then man intervened.

Roses

The earliest references to rose cultivation are found on clay tablets discovered in Iraq that date back to 2500 BCE. From Asia Minor, the crusades brought back the damask rose and the apothecary's rose. In the sixteenth century, the Dutch created the centifolia roses, then came the moss roses and most importantly, the repeat-flowering roses. In 1583, the first hybrid yellow rose appeared. The eighteenth century saw the first hybrid teas, the nineteenth century the Boursault and Noisette roses, then the Polyantha roses which, in the twentieth century, would be used to produce the Floribundas by crossing them with hybrid teas. Today, plant breeders continue to produce new varieties. The fashion is once again for fragrant varieties, such as those produced by David Austin for his English Roses collection, and by French breeders like the house of Meilland with their Romantica roses, the Guillot family with their Generosa roses and Delbard with its "Souvenirs d'Amour." Also much sought after are the disease-resistant varieties that require very little maintenance. The German rose breeder Kordes is one of the leaders in this field.

[left] 'Sourire d'Orchidée'.
[1] 'Veilchenblau'.
[2] 'Mme Alfred Carrière'.
[3] 'Graham Thomas', a very fragrant rose, created by David Austin.

1　2

3

[1] 'Pink Grootendorst.'
[2] 'Pierre de Ronsard.'
[3] 'Abraham Darby.'
[4] 'Winchester Cathedral.'
[5] 'American Pillar.'
[6] 'Reflets de Saint-Malo.'
[7] Rose de Puteaux.

197

[1] 'Colette.'
[2] 'Graham Thomas.'
[3] 'Claude Monet.'
[4] 'Parfum de l'Haÿ.'

[5] 'Mermaid.'
[6] 'Reflets de Saint-Malo.'
[7] Rose des Cisterciens.

[1] 'Carmagnole.'
[2] 'Dynasty.'

[3] 'Excelsa.'
[4] 'Iceberg.'
[5] 'Impératrice Farah.'

[1] China Rose (*Rosa chinensis* 'Mutabilis.')
[2] 'Yves Piaget.'
[3] 'Cuisse de Nymphe.'
[4] 'Comte de Chambord.'
[5] 'Bonica.'

Aperennial is a plant that lives for a number of years. With some perennials, the part above ground dies back in winter but re-emerges the following spring. Others remain visible all year round, having what are known as persistent leaves.

In temperate zones, the cycle followed by perennial plants is always the same. In spring, young shoots emerge from the soil; they are either produced from a seed that has germinated or grow directly from the base of the mother plant. The shoot grows, puts out leaves, and then blooms. The flowers are fertilized by the wind or by insects and the fruit forms, which contains the seed. Autumn arrives, the leaves turn yellow in deciduous species, and the ripe fruit falls to the ground or is carried away by birds. Surrounded by its own food source, the seed that has been released waits in the soil until spring arrives before germinating and producing a new plant. The mother plant also enters a period of rest and waits for the first warmth of spring before putting out new shoots. Some plants retain all or part of their foliage and their stem during the winter, others lose all parts above ground. Over time, perennials become bigger, growing into larger clumps and producing an increasing number of flowers. Often, during the first years of their life, they can appear frail, can be sensitive to cold and disease, and can refuse to flower. This is true of peonies, which can take as long as five years before they start to produce blooms. But good gardeners will see their patience rewarded and, as they reach maturity, perennials become increas-

Perennials

ingly beautiful and, most importantly, require almost no maintenance. Their lifespan varies considerably depending on the species. Some, like Himalayan poppies, have a very short lifespan of only three or four years; others, such as lupins, tend to deteriorate with age; while others, like sage, can continue to flourish for several hundred years.

[1] Yellow Archangel (*Lamium galeobdolon*) is a shade-loving plant.
[2] Mourning Widow (*Geranium phaeum*) can withstand cold temperatures.
[3] Navelwort 'Starry Eyes' (*Omphalodes cappadocica*).

[4] Daisy (*Bellis perennis*).
[5] The Chinese Peony (*Paeonia lactiflora*) has very fragrant flowers.
[6] Auricula Primula (*Primula auricula*).
[7] Foamflower (*Tiarella wherryi*), a small rockery plant.

[1] Anemone de Caen (*Anemone coronaria*), also known as the Florists' Anemone.
[2] Helenium 'Moerheim Beauty' (*Helenium hybrid*) enjoys a position in full sun.
[3] The Cinquefoil (*Potentilla nepalensis*) will grow at very high altitudes.
[right] Golden Cinquefoil (*Potentilla aurea*), a ground-covering rockery plant.

[1] Japanese Anemone (*Anemone hupehensis*) enjoys shade and damp.
[2] Yarrow 'Paprika' (*Achillea millefolium* hybrid).
[3] *Primula capitata*, also known as the Asiatic Primrose.

[4] Anemone de Caen (*Anemone coronaria*).
[5] *Salvia nemorosa* 'Schneehügel' prefers a shady position.
[6] The Michaelmas Daisy (*Aster novi-belgii*) flowers at the end of summer.
[7] The Virginia Spiderwort (*Tradescantia virginiana*) is a hardy perennial related to the houseplant Wandering Sailor.

[1] Hardy Geranium 'Johnson's Blue' (*Geranium hybrid*) produces one of the strongest blues.
[2] Gaillardia 'Royale' (*Gaillardia* x *grandiflora*).
[3] Pink (*Dianthus hybrid*).
[4] Japanese Anemone (*Anemone hupehensis*).
[5] Purple Coneflower (*Echinacea purpurea*).
[6] The Lupin (*Lupinus* x *polyphyllus*) is a hardy perennial but tends to deteriorate over the years.

An annual is a plant that germinates, flowers, bears fruit, and dies, all in a single season. In the garden, certain perennial species are treated as annuals. This is true of frost-sensitive plants such as pelargoniums.

In the wild, generally speaking, annuals tend to be modest flowerers, such as the grasses. Pollinated by the wind, they produce a very large quantity of seeds to ensure the survival of their species. Many are considered to be invasive, such as the pimpernel, which produces fruits resembling small boxes, the lids of

Annuals

which, when they open, release thousands of seeds. More than 500,000 of these seeds have been counted in an area of 120 sq. yd. (100 m^2)! Each of them remains able to germinate for several years, so the pimpernel can die content, knowing that its survival is assured. Many of the weeds that cause so many problems for gardeners are annuals.

Fortunately, other annuals are less prolific, and importantly, bear larger, more colorful flowers. Many of the perennials brought here from warmer regions with milder winters, and acclimatized to our part of the world, will behave like annuals. This is true of fuchsias, pelargoniums, and petunias. Although it is possible to keep them from

one year to the next by moving them to a dark, well-ventilated, frost-free place for the winter, they are usually replaced each spring by pot-grown plants bought in a garden center. Other species have a short life cycle that extends over two years: These are the biennials, which include larkspurs. They are usually planted out in summer to flower the following spring.

[1] Cut-leaf Daisy (*Brachyscome multifida*).
[2] Honeywort (*Cerinthe major* 'Purpurascens') has a tendency to self-seed.
[3] Gazania (*Gazania* hybrid).

[4] Fivespot (*Nemophila maculata*) – so named because of the marks on its petals.
[5] The Nasturtium (*Tropaeolum majus*) dies each year but reappears the following spring.
[6] Snapdragon (*Antirrhinum majus*).

[1] Honeywort (*Cerinthe major* 'Purpurascens.')
[2] Bacopa (*Sutera diffusa*) makes an excellent hanging plant.
[3] Bidens 'Golden Flame' (*Bidens ferulifolia*) needs full sunlight.
[4] and [5] Petunia (*Petunia* x *hybrida*), very easy to grow and tolerant of hot, dry conditions.

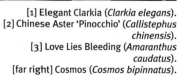

[1] Elegant Clarkia (*Clarkia elegans*).
[2] Chinese Aster 'Pinocchio' (*Callistephus chinensis*).
[3] Love Lies Bleeding (*Amaranthus caudatus*).
[far right] Cosmos (*Cosmos bipinnatus*).

[1] and [8] Mallow (*Lavatera trimestris*).
[2] *Diascia* hybrid.
[3] Amaranthus (*Amaranthus hybrid*) is popular in
dried flower arrangements.
[4] African Marigold (*Tagetes hybrida*).
[5] Snapdragon (*Antirrhinum majus*).
[6] Zinnia 'Pacific Yellow' (*Zinnia elegans*).
[7] Joseph's Coat (*Amaranthus tricolor*).

A mong the plants we grow in our gardens are the bulbous plants, including species that botanists divide into bulbs, tubers, corms, rhizomes, and plants with tuberous roots. There are more than 5,000 species of bulbous plants.

A true bulb is a miniature replica of the plant itself. If you cut it open you will find leaves wrapped tightly on top of one another, protecting a stem topped by a flower shoot. These leaves are known as "scales." They are fleshy because they contain the plant's food reserves. The whole thing is covered in a protective membrane called a "tunic." At the base of the bulb is a disc or "basal plate" from which the roots emerge. Narcissi and lilies grow from true bulbs.

Corms are the result of the swelling of the base of the flowering stem in which the food reserves will be stored. Cormous plants also have a "tunic" and a "plate" from which the roots emerge. Crocuses and gladioli grow from corms. Tubers are also a swelling of the flowering stem but they do not have a "tunic" or a "plate." Anemones and begonias form part of this group. Tuberous plants are those whose swollen roots store their food reserves in their tissue, such as dahlias and ranunculus.

Bulbous Plants

Rhizomes are formed by a thick stem that snakes its way along just under the surface of the soil. At intervals, the rhizome will produce buds consisting of scale leaves from which young, vertical shoots emerge. Cannas and lily-of-the-valley are plants with rhizomes. During their growing period, all these plants use these swollen parts to store their food supply.

[1] Amaryllis 'Double Picotee' (*Hippeastrum hybrid*).
[2] Dwarf Bearded Iris (*Iris pumila*). The flowers last only one day but continue to appear for several weeks.
[3] Hardy Cyclamen (*Cyclamen hederifolium*). Its flattened corms are poisonous.
[4] Hyacinth 'L'Innocence' (*Hyacinthus orientalis*). Its flowers are very fragrant in the evening.
[5] Spanish Iris 'White Ideal' (*Iris xiphium*).
[6] Summer Snowflake (*Leucojum aestivum*).
[7] Tuberous Begonia 'Crispa Marginata' (*Begonia* x *tuberhybrida*).
[8] Dahlia (*Dahlia* hybrid). Its tubers are edible.

[1] Amaryllis 'Stassen Glory' (*Hippeastrum* hybrid).
[2] Gladiolus (*Gladiolus* hybrid). This flower has an unfortunate reputation – in the language of flowers it signifies contempt.
[3] *Crocosmia* 'Lucifer'.
[4] Martagon Lily (*Lilium martagon*). This is a protected species.
[5] Turkistan Tulip (*Tulipa turkestanica*).
[6] Amaryllis 'Picotee' (*Hippeastrum* hybrid). The fine red edge on its petals makes it one of the most beautiful hybrids.
[7] Tuberous Begonia 'Crispa Marginata' (*Begonia* x *tuberhybrida*).

237

[left] Lily-Flowered Tulip (*Tulipa* hybrid).
[1] Belladonna Lily (*Amaryllis belladonna*). A bulbous plant native
to South Africa.
[2] Peacock or Tiger Flower (*Tigridia pavonia* 'Alba'). The flowers
last for only a few hours, but fresh ones appear each day.
[3] Tassel Hyacinth (*Muscari comosum*). Its small flowers smell of
heliotrope.

[1] Lily 'Carnaval' (*Lilium* hybrid).
[2] Regal Lily (*Lilium regale*). Its flowers are strongly scented, particularly in the evening.
[3] Dahlia (*Dahlia* hybrid).
[right] Bunch-flowered Narcissus (*Narcissus tazetta*). Its flowers are used in the manufacture of numerous perfumes.

Trees first appeared on Earth 250 million years ago and are the plant world's great innovators. They have given us seeds, fruits, and, above all, flowers. The ginkgo, the first tree to appear on our planet, still survives.

The trees that adorn our countryside, our gardens, and our towns also provide us with medicines such as quinine, food in the form of fruit, fragrances like ylang-ylang, dyes such as annatto, and resins such as myrrh and incense. Other trees like balsa, ebony, and oak are used in the construction of boats, houses, etc. Trees also provide food and shelter for birds, mammals, and insects. And finally, they provide the shade without which a multitude of species could not survive and without which the world would become a desert.

All trees – from the little arctic willow, which is only 1 in. (2.5 cm) high, to the giant California redwood – have one thing in common; they produce wood. Trees are ligneous plants, that is to say they produce lignite, a major constituent of wood. Which is why, as far as botanists are concerned, palm and banana trees are in fact not trees but grasses, whereas wisteria and even vines belong to the select club of trees and shrubs.

The term "tree" is generally reserved for species that possess a single trunk from

Flowering Trees

which boughs develop, which then give rise to branches from which new shoots develop, the whole thing forming the crown of the tree. The shape of the crown is particular to each species: auracarias are ovoid chestnuts and column shaped with a slightly rounded top; larches are arrow shaped; and African cedars and acacias are what is known as tabular in form.

[1] Japanese Pagoda Tree (*Sophora japonica*). Its honey-scented flowers bloom in late summer.
[2] Hazel (*Corylus avellana*). The catkins appear in the middle of winter.
[3] Pear Tree (*Pyrus communis*) and [4] Sweet Cherry (*Prunus* x *avium*). The flowers are fertilized by bees.

[5] Quince (*Cydonia vulgaris*). It has downy flower petals.
[6] Black Locust (*Robinia pseudoacacia*). Its flowers are used to make fritters.
[7] Bull Bay (*Magnolia grandiflora*).

[left] Sweet Chestnut (*Castanea sativa*). The honey produced from its flowers is very dark brown.
[1] Red Horse chestnut (*Aesculus* x *carnea*). Its flowers are sterile.
[2] Swamp Wattle (*Acacia retinodes*) is associated with the celebration of "grandmothers' day."
[3] Apple Tree (*Malus pumila*).

[1] Indian Bean Tree (*Catalpa bignonioides*). This tree is commonly planted in towns and cities.
[2] Lime Tree (*Tilia vulgaris*). The flowers make a soothing infusion.

[3] Common Walnut (*Juglans regia*). The small female flower gets pollen from the male catkin.
[4] Wild Service Tree (*Sorbus torminalis*). Its edible fruits are known as "checkers."
[5] Flowering Dogwood (*Cornus kousa*).

249

Flowering Trees

[1] and [2] Judas Tree (*Cercis siliquastrum*), so called because it was said that Judas hanged himself from this tree after betraying Jesus.

[3] The Medlar Tree (*Mespilus germanica*) produces the fruit known as medlars.

[4] The Silk Tree (*Albizia julibrissin*) is sensitive to cold, so better cultivated in frost-free areas.

[5] Magnolia Tree (*Magnolia* hybrid).

[6] The Rose Bay or Oleander (*Nerium oleander*) is a highly poisonous tree native to the Mediterranean.

251

[1] Tree of Heaven (*Ailanthus altissima*), is found in towns, on building sites and wasteland.
[2] Foxglove Tree (*Paulownia tomentosa*) is very common in large parks.
[3] Magnolia (*Magnolia* hybrid).
[4] Ornamental Cherry (*Prunus hybrid*). Clusters of blossoms appear before the leaves in spring.
[5] Elder (*Sambucus nigra*) often found growing close to houses.
[6] Common Walnut (*Juglans regia*), pollen-bearing male catkins.

I n the wild, shrubs often live in the shade of tall trees. And in cultivation, their abundant flowers and unobtrusive presence make them one of the essential structural elements of any pleasure garden.

Like trees, large and small shrubs produce wood. The dividing line between them is purely one of convention and has more to do with the form of the species than its height. Generally speaking, a small tree is around 23 ft. (7 m) tall, with a single, very short trunk. The term shrub describes a plant that produces a number of trunk-like stems from the base.

The branches of shrubs are often flexible and some, like roses, become climbers as they mature. Others, usually those native to mountain areas such as junipers and certain pines, grow into trailing plants or creepers. Many also have decorative foliage that may turn purple in autumn, or have variegated yellow and white leaves, such as certain spindle trees. Many species, such as cotoneasters, have persistent foliage, making them ideal for hedging or, in the case of box, for edging.

Flowering Shrubs

The vast majority of shrubs tolerate clipping: Some like box, sweet bay, laurustinus (viburnum) and cherry laurel provide excellent subjects for topiary and are found clipped into geometric or animal shapes. Pruning can also transform trees into shrubs. If the main stem is cut down to ground level, the plant will develop several new stems. This practice (known as pollarding) is commonly used with willows. Certain trees with distorted branches can also turn into strangely shaped shrubs.

[1] Deutzia (*Deutzia* x *magnifica* 'Staphyleoides').
[2] Guelder Rose (*Viburnum opulus*). Its red berries are poisonous.
[3] Forsythia (*Forsythia* hybrid), one of the first shrubs to flower in spring.
[4] Flowering Currant (*Ribes sanguineum*).
[5] Van Houtte Spirea (*Spiraea* x *vanhouttei*). This hybrid is one of the most floriferous.
[6] Mallow (*Lavatera* hybrid). The flowers are fertilized by bumblebees.

[1] European Spindle (*Euonymus europaeus*). Spindleberries are poisonous.
[2] Hydrangea 'Mont Aso' (*Hydrangea serrata*). Only the central flowers are fertile.
[3] Barberry (*Berberis* hybrid).
[4] Japanese Tree Peony 'Shichifukujin' (*Paeonia suffruticosa*).
[5] Himalayan Honeysuckle or Pheasant Berry (*Leycesteria formosa*). Its fruit is very popular with pheasants.
[6] Weigela (*Weigela* sp.).
[7] Lilac (*Syringa vulgaris*). Its fragrant flowers are best enjoyed at the end of the day.

[1] Tree Peony 'Fen Dan Bai' (*Paeonia suffruticos*a).
[2] Viburnum 'Watanabe' (*Viburnum plicatum*).
[3] Cherry Laurel (*Prunus laurocerasus*). An ideal plant for hedging, but it can soon become invasive; the fruits are poisonous.
[far right] Rhododendron (*Rhododendron* hybrid).

[1] The Hydrangea (*Hydrangea macrophylla*) enjoys acid soil.
[2] Witch Hazel (*Hamamelis virginiana*) flowers in the depths of winter.

[3] Hawthorn (*Crataegus oxyacantha*) flowers in spring.
[4] Oak-leaved Hydrangea (*Hydrangea quercifolia*).
[5] California Lilac (*Ceanothus caeruleus*) produces one of the most beautiful blues of all flowering shrubs.
[6] White Lilac (*Syringa vulgaris*) is more delicate and less fragrant than the Common Lilac.
[7] Mexican Orange Blossom (*Choisya ternata*). Its flowers smell of oranges.

Climbers

In order to climb, plants have adopted a number of strategies. In many (known as twining plants or vines), the main stems twist spirally around a support. Other put out aerial roots, suckers, crampons, or tendrils.

In twining species, as soon as a young shoot emerges, the growing tip begins to describe a circular movement in order to find a support to which to cling. This is true of climbers from hops to morning glory. Each species has its own rotational direction which remains the same regardless of the support. For example, Japanese wisteria twines in a clockwise direction, whereas Chinese wisteria twists the opposite way. Other species use tendrils, which are small filaments produced by the stems, leaves, and even the flowers which explore the space around them by describing an ellipse. As soon as the tendril touches a support, its tip grasps it and twists round it in a matter of seconds. Some highly developed tendrils are coiled like small springs to give them some degree of flexibility once they have attached themselves – bryony is one example. This group also includes the Virginia creeper, which is able to adapt its tendrils to the support available. When it comes into contact with a branch, the tendrils coil round in the normal fashion, but when it encounters a flat surface, the tips of the tendrils are transformed into small suckers that adhere, attaching the plant to the support.

Other climbers put out aerial roots along their stems, which then lodge in the smallest crevices. Ivy is a perfect example. The slightest roughness, the smallest gap between two stones, and it is able to attach itself by its roots and climb.

Finally, there are species that use their thorns to climb. Roses use their thorns as crampons to cling and gain height and can cover an entire wall or trellis.

[1] *Clematis montana*. This mountain species is one of the first to flower.
[2] *Mina lobata* is an annual that can climb up to 10 ft. (3 m) in a single season.
[3] Tuberous Nasturtium (*Tropaeolum tuberosum*). This plant has edible tubers.
[4] *Clematis florida* 'Sieboldii,' also known as the Passionflower Clematis.
[5] Black-eyed Susan (*Thunbergia alata*), so called because of the dark center of the corolla.
[6] Wattakaka or *Dregea sinensis* is an Asian species with very fragrant flowers.

[1] Flame Flower (*Tropaeolum speciosum*).
[2] Golden Hop (*Humulus lupulus* 'Aureus'). The cones are used to flavor beer.
[3] Trumpet Vine (*Campsis radicans*). The nectar in its flowers is much sought after by bumblebees.
[4] The Cup and Saucer Vine (*Cobaea scandens*) is an annual.
[5] Bougainvillea or Paper Flower (*Bougainvillea glabra*) is a plant commonly found in warm climates.
[6] Chinese Wisteria (*Wisteria sinensis*). With age, the stems become tightly entwined around their supports.
[7] The Chocolate Vine (*Akebia quinata*) produces two types of purple flowers: male and female.

[left] English Ivy (*Hedera helix*). Its flowers provide one of the year's last sources of pollen for bees.
[1] Black-eyed Susan (*Thunbergia alata*) – a white form.
[2] Bolivian Nasturtium (*Tropaeolum tricolor*) is a collector's nasturtium.
[3] Canary Creeper (*Tropaeolum peregrinum*) is an annual.

[1] Large-flowered Clematis 'Blue Light' (*Clematis* hybrid).
[2] The Blue Passionflower (*Passiflora caerulea*) is the only passionflower that is hardy in frost-prone areas.
[3] Hog Peanut (*Apios tuberosa*).
[4] Perfoliate Honeysuckle (*Lonicera caprifolium*) has flowers that are very fragrant in the middle of the day.

[5] Alpine Clematis (*Clematis alpina*). Its flowers never open fully.
[6] Clematis 'Rouge Cardinal' (*Clematis* hybrid).

5

6

Flowers of the
Imagination

Burning Pheasant's Eye (*Adonis flammea*).
According to legend, Venus fell in love with
Adonis after being struck by his arrow.

On every continent and in every culture, numerous flowers have been dedicated to the gods. The classical pantheon is rich in floral myths, as are Christianity and the civilizations of China and India.

Aphrodite fell madly in love with the handsome Adonis, son of Myrrha. Jealous of this love, Mars transformed himself into a boar and tore Adonis to pieces during a hunt in the forests on the slopes of Mount Lebanon. In desperation, the goddess changed the body of her beloved into an anemone and throughout antiquity this flower was associated with Aphrodite's passion for Adonis. Many Greek statues show the goddess clasping a bunch of anemones. Among the Romans, Aphrodite (known as Venus) was considered to be the original ancestor of all the Roman people.

When Christ died on the cross, the entire earth was plunged into immense sorrow. Only one tree remained unmoved: "I am righteous," it said, "my conduct has always been irreproachable; Jesus died for the guilty – let them mourn; as for me, why should I be sad?" A passing angel heard the tree and to punish it for its arrogance declared: "You selfish tree, as punishment for refusing to share in this grief, I condemn you, even on calm, sunny days, to shiver eternally with cold." The tree in question was the aspen.

In China, the goddess of the cinnamon tree often came to earth to listen to men talking. One evening, she came upon a passionate debate among some scholars. The most eloquent of them, and also the most handsome, was Tchin Chi-Yeng. With the help of the divinities of the clove and vanilla trees, she succeeded in becoming the young man's lover. However, he was already engaged and his betrothed, with the assistance of the greatest magician in the kingdom, managed to drive the intruder away. Defeated, the goddess was now only able to seduce men with her fragrance.

Flowers of the Gods

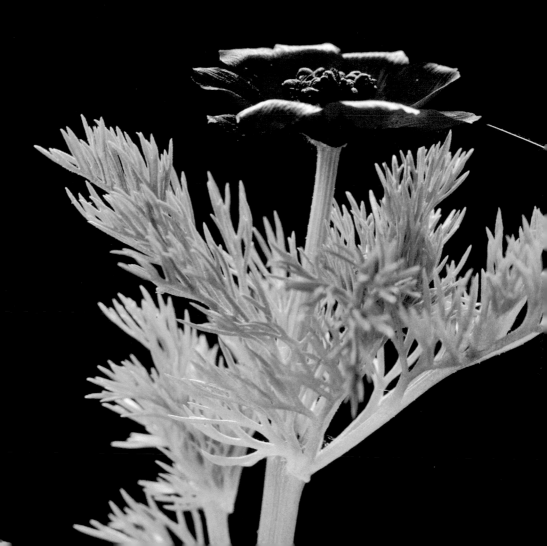

[1] Cannabis (*Cannabis sativa*). This plant was believed to allow people to contact the gods.
[2] and [3] Common Gorse (*Ulex europaeus*). Always in bloom, it was thought to be an incarnation of the devil.
[4] The Madonna Lily (*Lilium candidum*) is associated with the Virgin Mary.
[5] Tree Peony 'Shimane Chojuraku' (*Paeonia suffruticosa*).
[6] Protea (*Protea* sp.). The sea god Proteus was believed to be able to change his form at will, like the plants of this family.
[7] Chrysanthemum (*Chrysanthemum* hybrid).
[8] Victory Onion (*Allium victorialis*).

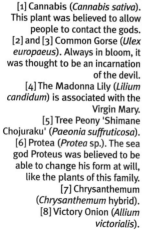

287

[1] Wild Daffodil (*Narcissus pseudonarcissus*).
[2] Lady's Slipper Orchid (*Cypripedium calceolus*). According to legend, when a human tried to get hold of Venus's Slipper, the goddess transformed herself into the orchid that now bears this name.
[3] Bunch-flowered Narcissus (*Narcissus tazetta*).

Flowers of the Gods

[4] The chrysanthemum (*Chrysanthemum* hybrid) is one of the four sacred plants of Japan, along with the plum tree, the bamboo, and the orchid.
[5] Cannabis (*Cannabis sativa*).
[6] Tree Peony 'Kokuryu Nishiki' (*Paeonia suffruticosa* hybrid). In China, for centuries the cultivation of these flowers was the sole preserve of emperors.

[far left] The Longbud Sugarbush (*Protea aurea*) is native to South Africa, as are all species of this genus.
[1] Madonna Lily *(Lilium candidum)*. The immaculate whiteness of its petals symbolizes the virginity of the Virgin Mary.
[2] Pheasant's Eye or Poet's Narcissus (*Narcissus poeticus*).
[3] Chrysanthemum 'Exotic Spider' (*Chrysanthemum* hybrid).

293

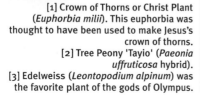

[1] Crown of Thorns or Christ Plant
(*Euphorbia milii*). This euphorbia was
thought to have been used to make Jesus's
crown of thorns.
[2] Tree Peony 'Tayio' (*Paeonia
uffruticosa* hybrid).
[3] Edelweiss (*Leontopodium alpinum*) was
the favorite plant of the gods of Olympus.

[4] Jerusalem Thorn (*Paliurus australis*). This spiny shrub was also believed to have pierced Jesus's forehead during his crucifixion.

[5] Peyote (Lophophora williamsii). The Aztecs communicated with their gods by chewing this small hallucinogenic cactus.

[6] Ragged Robin (*Lychnis flos-cuculi*).

[7] Asphodel (*Asphodelus albus*). Dedicated to Persephone, the goddess of the Underworld, this plant was believed to grow in the village of the dead.

Blood Lily (*Haemanthus* sp.). The bulbs of this plant are used in the practise of magic in South Africa, where their juice is poured into the eyes of participants during initiation ceremonies.

Plants provide us with substances that enable us to feed and heal ourselves. Some of them also possess strange properties than can transport the user into another, extraordinary world.

The countryside abounds in plants believed to protect us. Mistletoe and holly suspended from the dining room ceiling are supposed to guard against lightning, fire, and flood, as well as bad fortune, poor harvests, and infidelity. In some areas, a ball of mistletoe was always hung over the crib of newborn babies to stop fairies indulging in their favorite pastime – baby swapping.

Magic plants, and there were many of them, were also believed to protect against the devil. Flax is one of the best known. To drive a demon from a house, one simply had to prepare two small bags, one filled with cayenne pepper and the other with blue flax flowers. The contents of each bag were then thrown in alternate handfuls against the walls while crying "For the red bishop!" when throwing the pepper and "For the devil!" when throwing the flax flowers.

Flowers were – and still are – an essential part of love and fertility rites. Saffron, mandrake, and ginseng were all reputed to be strongly aphrodisiac. Conversely, the chaste tree and lettuce were thought to calm the strongest passions. In Belgium, an ancient tradition still takes place. Young

Magic Plants

girls of marrying age gather in a circle around a large sheet of paper with a primrose flower in the center. The paper is then tossed until the flower falls from it and it is said that the girl standing on the side where the flower lands will marry within the year. If the flower falls the right way up her husband will be trustworthy and will make her happy; if it falls upside down, he will be a scoundrel who will regularly cheat on her!

[1] Purple Betony (*Stachys officinalis*) is believed to protect those out at night from spells and danger.

[2] The Houseleek (*Sempervivum tectorum*) was believed to offer protection from the devil.

[3] Mouse-ear Hawkweed (*Hieracium pilosella*).

[4] Avens (*Geum* hybrid).

[5] Blood Lily (*Haemanthus canaliculus*).

[6] China Aster (*Callistephus chinensis*). This plant was a common sight in priest's gardens. In the Christian tradition, it is associated with the ascension of the Virgin Mary because it flowers around August 15th.

[7] Artichoke (*Cynara scolymus*). Its flowers are reputed to be highly aphrodisiac.

[8] *Desfontainea spinosa*. Using an infusion made from the leaves of this plant, the shamans of the Kamba tribe of Colombia predict the future and identify illnesses.

[1] and [5] Kidney Vetch (*Anthyllis vulneraria*). An infusion made from its flowers was believed to heal arrow wounds. [2] Wormwood (*Artemisia vulgaris*). In the countryside, women were careful not to touch this plant as it was believed to cause miscarriages.

[3] Spiny Restharrow
(*Ononis spinosa*).
[4] Blessed Thistle (*Cnicus benedictus*). In the Middle Ages, this plant was believed to have miraculous properties, hence its common name.
[6] Blood lily (*Haemanthus albiflos*).

[left] Acanthus-leaved Thistle
(*Carlina acanthifolia*).
[1] Butterfly Pea (*Clitoria ternata*).
[2] Wormwood (*Artemisia vulgaris*).
[3] Mountain Houseleek (*Sempervivum montanum*).

305

[1] Lady's Mantle (*Alchemilla mollis*). The droplets found on its leaves were collected by sorcerers.
[2] Creeping Cinquefoil (*Potentilla reptans*), with five sepals, five petals, five leaves. The repetition of this sacred number is believed to bring Love, Money, Power, Health, and Wisdom. It is enough to carry it on one's person to obtain everything one desires.
[3] Chinese Aster (*Callistephus chinensis*).
[4] Holy Basil (*Ocimum sanctum*).
[5] Holly (*Ilex aquifolium*). In the past, young girls would tell what their future held in store by counting the spikes on holly leaves while reciting spinster, wife, widow, nun....

3

4

5

Linnaeus noticed that flowers of the same species open and close every day at the same time. More surprising still, even when picked they followed the same pattern as those still growing in the soil. This led him to devise his flower clock.

Using this clock, it is possible to work out the time of day by following the pattern of flowers opening and closing. For example, when the huge, white, fragrant flowers of the queen of the night close, it is midnight. Certain other species close even later; the moonflower closes its corolla at 1:00 am and the geranium triste at 2:00 am. One of the first flowers to open is the bindweed, at 3:00 am, closely followed by the meadow salsify (Jack-go-to-bed-at-noon). Around 5:00 am, the blue flowers of the chicory plant open, followed around 6:00 am by the ox tongue. At 7:00 am there is a general awakening that includes the mouse-ear hawkweed, the sow thistle, and the white water lily. At 8:00 am it is the turn of the scarlet pimpernel and the marigold. At 10:00 am, when the chicory, lettuce, and sow thistle are closing, the ice plant is beginning to open its dew-covered flowers. Around 11:00 am, it is the turn of the hawksbeard to close and the mesembryanthemum to open, and at 11:00 am it is also time for the star of Bethlehem to awake. At 1:00 pm the dandelion opens its yellow corolla and the proliferous pink closes. The scilla waits until 2:00 pm to open and at 3:00 pm it is time for the hawkweed, the St. Bernard's lily, and the ice plant to close. At 4:00 pm it is the turn of

Linnaeus's Clock

the alyssum. At 5:00 pm the first nocturnal flowers begin to open, such as the moonflower and the night-flowering catchfly. Then at 6:00 pm the geranium triste closes, followed at 7:00 pm by the scilla. At 8:00 pm the Mediterranean catchfly opens its corolla. And the day comes to an end with the plant that began it: the queen of the night.

1

2

[1] Common Chicory (*Cichorium intybus*) – its flowers open at 5:00 am and close at 10:00 am.
[2] White Campion (*Melandrium album*) opens at 5:00 pm.
[3] and [5] Star of Bethlehem (*Ornithogalum umbellatum*) opens at 11:00 am.
[4] Queen of the Night (*Selenicereus grandiflorus*) opens at 10:00 pm and closes at midnight.
[6] Dandelion (*Taraxacum densleonis*) opens at 1:00 pm.
[7] Ice Plant (*Mesembryanthemum cristallinum*) opens at 10:00 am and closes at 3:00 pm.

[1] Sweet Alyssum (*Alyssum maritimum*) opens at 11:00 am.
[2] St. Bernard's Lily (*Phalangium liliago*) closes at 3:00 pm.
[3] and [4] Scarlet Pimpernel (*Anagallis arvensis*). This plant usually produces orange flowers but more rarely produces blue ones.
[5] Ice Plant (*Mesembryanthemum cristallinum*).
[6] The European White Waterlily (*Nymphaea alba*) opens at 7:00 am but closes if a storm threatens.

[1] and [2] Marvel of Peru or Moonflower (*Mirabilis jalapa*). Its fragrant flowers open at 5:00 pm.
[3] Field Marigold (*Calendula arvensis*) opens at 8:00 am.
[4] Field Bindweed (*Convolvulus arvensis*) opens at 3:00 am by untwisting its flowers.
[right] The Day Lily (*Hemerocallis* sp.) opens at midday and closes at 8:00 pm.

[1] The Alpine Squill (*Scilla bifolia*) opens at 2:00 pm.
[2], [4], and [5] Day Lily (*Hemerocallis sp.*). The flowers
last for only one day but new ones open every day.
[3] Queen of the Night (*Selenicereus grandiflorus*)
waits for nightfall before opening.

The language of flowers originated in harems where eunuchs became the bearers of messages of love expressed through flowers. In the eighteenth century, Europe adopted this language and lovers used it to declare their passion.

Throughout the world, celebrations, births, marriages, and deaths are occasions marked by the giving of flowers. Indian temples are strewn with lotus and jasmine flowers which are replaced fresh every day; when the League of Nations building was inaugurated, it was covered with more than 50,000 roses donated by the Agha Khan; and the sea was strewn with thousands of red and white carnations for the marriage of Grace Kelly and Prince Rainier of Monaco, testimony to the importance flowers play in mankind's tradition and culture.

Each flower has its own symbolism, which can vary according to country, region, color, and number. Giving flowers has become a kind of coded language that obeys very precise rules worth knowing.

By giving a camellia, a suitor was declaring "You are the most beautiful." If the young girl in question were to place a hyacinth at her window, the response was: "A favorable omen." The lover could then respond by giving asters, meaning "Believe in me"; or wallflowers, meaning "My heart is true"; verbena, meaning "Do not abandon me for another"; or violets, meaning "I'm thinking of you." The young girl could then continue this dialogue by

The Language of Flowers

offering lilies, meaning "My feelings are pure"; or snowdrops, meaning "You are my first love." If a man received a bouquet of water lilies, it signified "You are a bad lover," while cut rosemary meant "I dismiss you," and narcissi meant "You are too proud." For women, a bouquet of amaryllis meant "You are a coquette," and cherry blossom meant "You are lazy."

[1] Sweet Violet (*Viola odorata*). This is the flower of modesty, but also of submission.
[2] Rose (*Rosa* hybrid). To give someone a bunch of roses of different colors is a sign of courtesy.
[3] Sweet William (*Dianthus barbatus*). This flower means: burning love; I am your slave.
[4] Common Bugloss (*Anchusa officinalis*) means: you are deceiving me.
[5] Cuckoo Flower (*Cardamine pratensis*) means: paternal error.
[6] Wallflower (*Erysimum* hybrid) means: constancy, faithfulness in adversity, lasting beauty.
[7] Ox-eye Daisy (*Leucanthemum vulgare*). Traditionally, the petals are pulled off one at a time while reciting "He loves me, he loves me not"...to find out which statement is true.

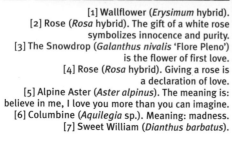

[1] Wallflower (*Erysimum* hybrid).
[2] Rose (*Rosa* hybrid). The gift of a white rose
symbolizes innocence and purity.
[3] The Snowdrop (*Galanthus nivalis* 'Flore Pleno')
is the flower of first love.
[4] Rose (*Rosa* hybrid). Giving a rose is
a declaration of love.
[5] Alpine Aster (*Aster alpinus*). The meaning is:
believe in me, I love you more than you can imagine.
[6] Columbine (*Aquilegia* sp.). Meaning: madness.
[7] Sweet William (*Dianthus barbatus*).

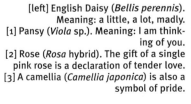

[left] English Daisy (*Bellis perennis*).
Meaning: a little, a lot, madly.
[1] Pansy (*Viola* sp.). Meaning: I am thinking of you.
[2] Rose (*Rosa* hybrid). The gift of a single
pink rose is a declaration of tender love.
[3] A camellia (*Camellia japonica*) is also a
symbol of pride.

1

2

3

[1] Ox-eye Daisy (*Leucanthemum vulgare*).
[2] Rose (*Rosa* hybrid). The gift of a yellow
rose is a sign of scorn or a way of rejecting
an over-eager lover.
[3] Michaelmas Daisy (*Aster novi-belgii*).
[4] The Hyacinth (*Hyacinthus orientalis*)
signifies the pain of love.
[5] The Giant Bellflower (*Campanula
latifolia*) is a sign of submission.
[6] Columbine (*Aquilegia vulgaris*).
[7] The Hawthorn (*Crataegus oxyacantha*)
means prudence, gentle hope, conceal
your love.

333

For French revolutionaries it was unacceptable that the days of the year be associated with religious images. The saints' calendar was replaced with flowers, fruit, vegetables, minerals, tools, and animals.

The year was divided into twelve equal months of thirty days to which five days had to be added that did not belong to any month and were known as "additional days." Each month was divided into three equal parts of ten days each, known as "decades." To name the months of the year, French revolutionaries turned to agricultural symbolism. So the autumn months were called "vendémiaire" (meaning wine harvest), "brumaire" (mist), and "frimaire" (wintry weather); the winter months were "nivôse" (snow), "pluviôse" (rain), and "ventôse" (wind); the spring months were "germinal" (seed), "floréal" (flower) and "prairial" (meadow); and the summer months were "messidor" (harvest),

"thermidor" (gift of warmth), and "fructidor" (fruit). Each day was associated with a seasonal flower, fruit, or vegetable—except the fifth day, which was associated with an animal; the tenth day, associated with a tool; and the whole of "nivôse" (1 to 21 December), each day of which was associated with a mineral.

The poet Fabre d'Églantine took on the task of finding the appropriate match. Thus, for the first decade of "vendémiaire" (1 to 22 September) he decided upon: 1 (primedi): grape; 2 (duodi): saffron; 3 (tridi): sweet chestnut; 4 (quartidi): autumn

Revolutionary Flowers

crocus; 5 (quintidi): horse; 6 (sextidi): balsam; 7 (septidi): carrot; 8 (octidi): amaranth; 9 (nonidi): parsnip; 10 (decadi): vat. However, the revolutionary (or republican) calendar never really caught on.

It remained in official use until the beginning of the "Empire." On January 1, 1806, the Gregorian calendar returned and with it, the saints.

[1] Angelica (*Angelica archangelica*): Prairial 04.
[2] European Teasel (*Dipsacus silvestris*): Fructidor 17.
[3] Wormwood (*Artemisia absinthium*): Messidor 09.
[4] Comfrey (*Symphytum officinale*): Floréal 16.
[5] Fly Honeysuckle (*Lonicera xylosteum*): Floréal 14.
[6] Heather (*Calluna vulgaris*): Frimaire 22.

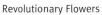

Revolutionary Flowers

3

4

6

5

337

[1] Large Periwinkle (*Vinca major*): Germinal 11.
[2] Wild Mignonette (*Reseda lutea*): Vendémiaire 14.
[3] Evergreen Candytuft (*Iberis sempervirens*): Pluviôse 21.

[4] Woodland Strawberry
(*Fragaria vesca*): Prairial 11.
[5] Coltsfoot (*Tussilago farfara*):
Ventôse 01.

341

[far left] Great Burnet (*Sanguisorba officinalis*): Floréal 17.
[1] Valerian (*Valeriana officinalis*): Floréal 24.
[2] Chamomile (*Matricaria chamomilla*): Prairial 22.
[3] Dog Rose (*Rosa canina*): Fructidor 21.

[1] Germander Speedwell
(*Veronica chamaedrys*):
Messidor 4.
[2] Spurge Laurel (*Daphne
laureola*): Pluviôse 1.
[3] Rampion Bellflower
(*Campanula rapunculus*):
Frimaire 1.

[4] True Lavender (*Lavandula angustifolia*):
Messidor 14.
[5] Plantain Leopardbane (*Doronicum plantagineum*): Ventôse 17.

[1] Borage (*Borago officinalis*):
Floréal 23.
[2] Sage (*Salvia officinalis*):
Messidor 26.
[3] Privet (*Ligustrum vulgare*):
Ventôse 04.
[4] Hardy Cyclamen (*Cyclamen hederifolium*): Pluviôse 28.

[5] Lungwort (*Pulmonaria officinalis*): Pluviôse 19.
[6] Cowslip (*Primula officinalis*): Germinal 01.
[7] Rhubarb (*Rheum rhaponticum*): Floréal 11.

Plant symbolism is also found on the emblems of towns, cities, regions, nations, and even companies. Plants appear on flags, coats of arms, and even on sportswear.

The pomegranate tree is the symbol of many Masonic lodges: Its plentiful seeds represent the fact that freemasons are found the whole world over. The olive tree is the emblem of the United Nations: it represents wisdom and peace. The shamrock is the emblem of Ireland: St. Patrick was said to have evangelized the country using the three-leaved shamrock to explain the Holy Trinity. The lily is the symbol of French royalty; however, the stylized version used to decorate royal coats of arms is in fact a yellow iris. According to legend, when Clovis, king of the Franks, found himself in a serious plight during the battle of Tolbiac he spotted some yellow irises growing in the middle of a river; this meant that there was a ford where he could cross the river and pursue the enemy (this type of iris grows only in shallow water). Once the battle was won, he replaced the three toads on his banner with three irises. During Louis VII's crusade, this new royal emblem became Louis's floral banner and was stylized to become the "fleur de lis." Many years later, Josephine made Napoleon a gift of violets when they first met and the violet thus became the symbol of the first Empire.

Coats of arms abound in representations of plants and flowers. The ash and the marigold are common features. The ash symbolizes greatness and friendship – no snake will rest in the shade of the ash tree;

Flower Emblems

and the marigold symbolizes power – its yellow flowers embody the sun. Many towns, cities, and countries have also chosen plants as their emblem: Quimper has the elder, Canada the maple leaf, Lebanon the cedar tree, Wales the daffodil and leek, and England the rose. The rose is also the emblem of Bulgaria, Finland, Iraq, the Maldives, Romania, and Georgia.

350

[1] and [3] Peruvian Lily (*Alstroemeria aurantiaca*). This is the national flower of Patagonia.

[2] The Toad Lily (*Trillium sessile*) is the emblem of Quebec.

[4] The Pasque Flower (*Pulsatilla vulgaris*) is the emblem of the Canadian province of Manitoba. [5] The Violet (*Viola* sp.) is the emblem of the Napoleonic Empire.

[6] The Bearded Iris (*Iris germanica*) is the emblem of Tennessee.

[7] *Cattleya* sp. This orchid is the emblem of several countries, including Costa Rica.

[8] The Wild Tulip (*Tulipa sylvestris*) is the national flower of Iran.

[1] *Disa uniflora*. This orchid is the emblem of Cape Province, South Africa.
[2] Broom (*Sarothamnus scoparius*) is the emblem of the dukes of Anjou, France.
[3] The Cockspur Coral Tree (*Erythrina crista-galli*) is the emblem of Argentina.
[4] The Hibiscus (*Hibiscus rosa-sinensis*) is the national plant of South Korea.
[5] The Woolly Thistle (*Cirsium eriophorum*) is the emblem of Scotland.
[6] *Dendrobium phalaenopsis*, the Cooktown Orchid, is the floral emblem of Queensland, Australia.
[7] The 'York and Lancaster' Rose (*Rosa* hybrid) is the national flower of England.

[left] The Dahlia (*Dahlia* hybrid) is the emblem of Colorado.
[1] The Fringed Tulip (*Tulipa* hybrid) is the national flower of the Netherlands.
[2] The Yellow Flag (*Iris pseudacorus*) has been the emblem of the kings of France since the time of Clovis, the first king of the Franks.
[3] The Acanthus (*Acanthus mollis*) was the emblem of the Roman legions.

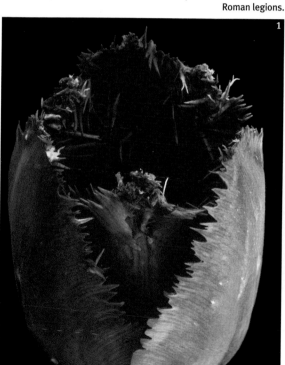

357

[1] The Dasystemon Tulip (*Tulipa tarda*) is the emblem of the city of Ottawa.
[2] The California Poppy (*Eschscholzia californica*) is the emblem of California.
[3] The Acanthus (*Acanthus mollis*) is also the emblem of the French national police academy.
[4] The Garland Chrysanthemum (*Chrysanthemum coronarium*) is the symbol of the Japanese imperial family.
[5] The German Iris (*Iris germanica*) is the emblem of the city of Brussels.

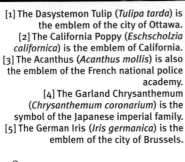

3

4

5

The Dahlia (*Dahlia* hybrid) is the good-luck plant for the month of October.

E ach of us is assigned three flowers for good luck: a birthday flower, a flower for the month of our birth, and a flower for the patron saint whose name we bear. Though considered a Christian tradition, it in fact dates back to ancient Rome.

A young woman called Mathilde and born on August 2nd will have the following floral "godparents": the Alpine snowbell for her saint, the tiger lily for the day she was born, and the gladiolus for her birth month. A boy named Valentine and born on February 18th will have the spring crocus, veronica, and primrose as his good-luck flowers. Those fortunate enough to be called Genevieve or Octavian are respectively associated with the iris and the rose. Less fortunate, however, are those born on January 5th or April 17th whose respective birth flowers are the fetid hellebore and the wild arum.

The Days in Flowers

The floral calendar familiar to us today dates back to 1870. It was created by Baron de Reinsberg-Düringsfeld from oral tradition and ancient books and contains some very familiar flowers, such as the field poppy and heather, but also species such as the hairy sphenogyne, unfamiliar to all but a handful of botanists. As the floral year progresses, we also find mosses, ferns, fungi, and some exotics such as the passionflower. These flowers do not appear to be linked to the seasons and it is hard to find a connection between them and the saints they represent. Only those associated with the months follow the pattern of the seasons they represent: January: snowdrop; February: primrose; March: daffodil; April: daisy; May: lily of the valley; June: rose; July: lily; August: gladiolus; September: aster; October: dahlia; November: chrysanthemum; December: holly.

[1] Purple Loosestrife (*Lythrum salicaria*) is associated with July 27th.
[2] The Autumn Crocus (*Colchicum autumnale*) is associated with September 10th and August 6th.

362

[3] and [7] Dahlia (*Dahlia* hybrid), October.
[4] The Tulip (*Tulipa* hybrid) is associated with March 17th.
[5] and [6] Spring Crocus (*Crocus vernus*), associated with
February 28th and February 14th.
[8] The German Iris (*Iris germanica*) is associated with May 12th.

[1] Deadnettle *(Lamium maculatum)* is associated with January 16th.
[2] Chamomile *(Matricaria chamomilla)* is associated with July 26th.
[3] and [5] Primulas *(Primula* sp.) are associated with the month of February.
[4] The Germander Speedwell *(Veronica chamaedrys)* is associated with February 18th.

[1] Sneezeweed (*Helenium autumnale*) is associated with October 3rd and October 13th.
[2] The Spear Thistle (*Cirsium lanceolatum*) is associated with August 3rd.
[3] The Prickly Poppy (*Argemone munita*) is associated with May 17th.
[right] The Calla Lily (*Zantedeschia hybrid*) is associated with April 17th.

[1] The Tiger Lily (*Lilium tigrinum*) is associated with August 2nd.
[2] Orange Hawkweed (*Hieracium aurantiacum*) is associated with July 19th.
[3] The Calla Lily (*Zantedeschia* hybrid) is associated with April 17th.
[4] and [6] Gladioli (*Gladiolus* hybrid) are associated with the month of August.
[5] The Auricula (*Primula auricula*) is associated with the month of February.
[7] The Cornflower (*Centaurea cyanus*) is associated with June 28th.

The Days in Flowers

5 6 7

Flowers
in Extreme
Habitats

Succulents have mastered the art of living in desert areas. Their thick stems and leaves are capable of storing water in their tissues, allowing the plants to survive very long periods of drought.

California is home to some curious species of plants. The great majority belong to the cactus family. These plants, which can wait for years for the smallest drop of water, have a heavily branching root system that enables them to take advantage of the slightest humidity. When a storm eventually occurs, the water taken up by the roots is transported throughout the plant by a system of interconnected ligneous channels. The cactus tissue swells and their stems become distended. The largest species, such as the cardon cactus, are able to store several tons of water in this way. Because pollinating insects are not common, cactus flowers tend to be very ostentatious. Producing these large, color-

Desert Flowers

ful petals requires a huge expenditure of energy, particularly in this hot climate – which is why the flowers last for only a few hours. Other species are also perfectly adapted to cope with water shortages, such as the elephant tree which can survive total drought for many months or even years. When a storm eventually breaks, the tree seems to come to life and is immediately covered in small green leaves, followed the next day by an abundance of red flowers that quickly fade to produce fruit and then seeds. In South Africa, hawthornias are able to withstand evaporation by burying themselves. When there is a drought, their fleshy roots contract and literally suck the plant into the sand. Only the tips of its leaves remain visible on the surface. As soon as it rains, the roots swell and the hawthornia resurfaces.

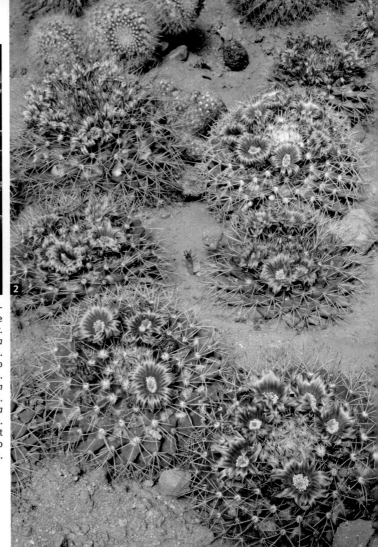

[1] Rose Cactus (*Pereskia grandiflora*). Its edible fruit are pear-shaped and angular.
[2] Mammillaria (*Mammillaria euthele*).
[3] *Rebutia muscula* is native to Bolivia.
[4] Desert Rose (*Adenium obesum*).
[5] The Opuntia (*Opuntia vestita*) produces edible fruit.
[6] The Stone Mimicry Plant (*Pleiospilos bolusii*) is native to South Africa.

[far left] Mariposa Lily (*Calochortus leichtlinii*).
[1] Indian Fig Opuntia (*Opuntia ficus-indica*). Its fruit is the prickly pear.
[2] *Calochortus leichtlinii* grows in the deserts of North America. It is the emblem of Utah.
[3] Saucer Plant (*Aeonium undulatum*).

[1] *Caralluma burchardii* is native to the Canary Islands.
[2] *Faucaria tigrina* is native to South Africa.
[3] The Hedgehog Cactus (*Echinocereus roetteri*) is native to Mexico.
[4] *Echinopsis silvestrii* is often called the Sea Urchin Cactus.

[5] The Hottentot Fig
(*Carpobrotus edulis*) is also
known as the Sour Fig
or Cape Fig.
[6] *Seticereus isagonus.*

[1] *Trichocereus* sp.
[2] Comb Hedgehog (*Echinocereus pectinatus*). The juicy fruit of this plant are edible and can be eaten fresh, along with their seeds.
[3] Mammillaria (*Mammillaria centricirrha*).
[far right] Red Crown Cactus (*Rebutia senilis* 'Stueneri').

[1] *Rebutia cintiensis*, native to Argentina.
[2] Mammillaria (*Mammillaria matudae*).
[3] Hedgehog Cactus (*Echinocereus reichenbachii*).
[4] Torch Cereus (*Trichocereus spachianus*).
[5] *Echinofossulocactus hastatus* is native to Mexico.
[6] The Krantz Aloe (*Aloe arborescens*) is native to South Africa.

[7] Sugared Almond Plant (*Pachyphytum oviferum*). Its succulent leaves covered in a whitish bloom have earned it the name "moonstones."

Species that have adapted to grow at high altitudes have done so by modifying their form, leaves, stems, and flowers in order to withstand the extreme cold and ultraviolet-rich light found at high elevations.

A low, carpeting habit is typical of plants that grow at high altitudes since, in addition to the cold, they also have to cope with fierce winds. Other species surround themselves with a protective, downy covering, such as edelweiss which is found in the Alps, and saussureas, found in the Himalayas, which wrap themselves in a transparent gauze. Dryads, on the other hand, take advantage of the heat of the sun to keep themselves warm. Their white corollas, shaped like concave mirrors, turn with the sun, directing its rays straight into the center of the flower, where the plant's reproductive organs are located. The temperature difference between the inside of the corolla and the outside can be more than 68°F (20°C). This curious plant "stove" is a delight for insects who come there to warm themselves up.

Because of its reflective qualities, white is one of the most common colors found in high altitude plants. The other color popular with flowers that live in cold regions is blue, since it is the most attractive color to pollinators. As insects are rare in such areas, it is important that a plant's powers of attraction are as great as possible. Himalayan poppies and gentians are among the most beautiful of all blue flowers. And the color gains in intensity the higher the altitude. To protect themselves from cold some species grow together in

Mountain Flowers

tightly knit groups, spending the winter in the shelter of rocks; this is true of saxifrages, which form large, moss-like clumps. Others, such as the bearded bellflower, never open their flowers and are therefore self-fertilizing. And others, such as hellebores, retain their leaves in winter, the leaves closing in around the fruit to form a protective coat.

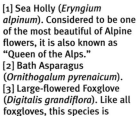

[1] Sea Holly (*Eryngium alpinum*). Considered to be one of the most beautiful of Alpine flowers, it is also known as "Queen of the Alps."
[2] Bath Asparagus (*Ornithogalum pyrenaicum*).
[3] Large-flowered Foxglove (*Digitalis grandiflora*). Like all foxgloves, this species is poisonous.
[4] Balloon Flower (*Platycodon grandiflorum*).

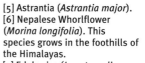

[5] Astrantia (*Astrantia major*).
[6] Nepalese Whorlflower
(*Morina longifolia*). This
species grows in the foothills of
the Himalayas.
[7] Edelweiss (*Leontopodium
alpinum*). Frequent picking has
now made this an endangered
species.

[1] Pyrenean Germander (*Teucrium pyrenaicum*).
[2] Alpine Sea Holly (*Eryngium alpinum*).
[3] Pyrenean Sea Holly (*Eryngium bourgatii*) is the Pyrenean equivalent of Alpine Sea Holly.
[4] Spiny Thistle (*Cirsium spinosissimum*).
[5] Great Yellow Gentian (*Gentiana lutea*). The root is used in the manufacture of alcoholic drinks.
[6] Alpine Erigeron (*Erigeron alpinus*).
[7] Sulfur-colored Windflower (*Anemone sulphurea*).

[Left page] Himalayan Blue Poppy (*Meconopsis betonicifolia*). High altitudes are rich in ultraviolet light and flowers are often a very pure blue.
[1] Musk Thistle or Nodding Thistle (*Carduus nutans*).
[2] White Hellebore (*Veratrum album*). Also known as the "False Helleborine," this plant is poisonous.
[3] Alpine Forget-Me-Not (*Myosotis alpestris*).

[1] Mountain Sandwort (*Arenaria montana*) grows among mountain scree.
[2] The Himalayan Gentian (*Gentiana cachemirica*) grows right along the Himalayas.
[3] Sulfur-colored Windflower (*Anemone sulphurea*).
[4] Musk Thistle or Nodding Thistle (*Carduus nutans*).
[5] Purple Gentian (*Gentiana purpurea*). Its flowers never open so it is self-fertilizing.
[6] The Glacier Crowfoot (*Ranunculus glacialis*) grows in the hollows of rocks at altitudes of up to 11,000 ft. (3,300 m).
[7] Alpine Toadflax (*Linaria alpina*).

A quarter of a million species of flowers have been recorded but scientists believe that this represents less than a tenth of the flora in existence. Unfortunately, many of them disappear before they are ever discovered.

Many species are lost from our planet every day. Some, like sandalwood, are exploited by man for their properties; others, like orchids, are picked for their beauty; some, like the cornflower and corncockle, are wiped out by the spread of agriculture; or, like peat bog flowers, by the destruction of their biotope. The orchid family is one of the most seriously affected. The lady's slipper orchid has long been the victim of its own beauty. Constant picking has made it necessary to take draconian measures: In some regions of Switzerland, a decision has even been taken to cut the flower stem as soon as it appears, the idea being that if its exquisite flower is not seen, the orchid will not be pulled up. Another plant family that is equally under threat is the bamboos.

Bamboos have a very unusual way of flowering. Although, of the hundreds of species worldwide, some flower regularly, the majority only flower once every twenty, or even sixty years. In fact, the square bamboo has never been seen in flower. These long intervals are accompanied by an astonishing phenomenon: All plants of the same species flower at the same time. This means that a plantlet growing in Europe will be in flower at the same time as its parent plant on the other side of the world! Although such flowering occurs only

Endangered Flowers

extremely rarely, when it does it is nonetheless abundant – and the enormous effort involved generally leads to the death of the plant. It is therefore essential that the precious, wind-borne pollen encounters female flowers so that they become fertilized. And this underlines the importance of mankind preserving the plant's natural habitat rather than destroying it.

[1] *Dendrobium antennatum.*
[2] *Dendrobium draconis.*
[3] The Sea Daffodil
(*Pancratium maritimum*)
is severely endangered,
as it grows on fine-sand
beaches popular with bathers
who trample the plants
or pull them up.

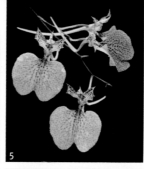

[4] *Phaius tankervilleae.*
[5] *Comparettia macroplectron.*
[6] *Brassavola martiana*, known as the "Lady of the Night Orchid" because it is most fragrant after nightfall.
[7] *Cirrhopetalum lepidum.*
[8] *Dendrobium miyakei.*

[1] The Corsican Hellebore (*Helleborus corsicus*) is endemic to the island of Corsica.
[2] *Paphiopedilum callosum*.
[3] *Paphiopedilum hirsutissimum*.
[4] The Yellow Geiger (*Cordia lutea*) is endemic to the Galapagos Islands.

[5] The Summer Snowflake (*Leucojum aestivum*) is now almost exclusively a cultivated plant.
[6] Spotted Gentian (*Gentiana punctata*).
[7] *Paphiopedilum fairieanum*.

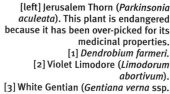

[left] Jerusalem Thorn (*Parkinsonia aculeata*). This plant is endangered because it has been over-picked for its medicinal properties.
[1] *Dendrobium farmeri.*
[2] Violet Limodore (*Limodorum abortivum*).
[3] White Gentian (*Gentiana verna* ssp. *alba*). This white form is only found on the Burren limestone plateau in Ireland.
[4] Corsican Crocus (*Colchicum corsicum*).

[1] *Neomoorea irrorata.*
[2] Round-leaved Wintergreen (*Pyrola rotundifolia*).
[3] *Espeletia grandiflora.*
[4] Common Twayblade (*Listera ovata*).
[5] *Dendrobium atroviolaceum.*
[6] *Oerstedella centradenia.*
[7] *Epidendrim ilense.* Only three specimens of this orchid have been found in the wild. It once grew in a forest in Ecuador that has now been destroyed. One of these plants was collected and increased in France, thus saving the species.

413

Water-loving Plants

By transforming their leaves into floats and extending their flowers up above the water, aquatic plants have managed to conquer an environment that is hostile to most other species. Indeed, water has even become their means of reproduction.

In the still backwaters of the Amazon, the flower of a water lily, with giant leaves over 3 ft. (1 m) in diameter, opens in the late afternoon. White and fragrant, it attracts large cockchafers seeking out pollen to eat, but its anthers remain tightly shut. The flower closes back over them, imprisoning its hungry visitors. All day long, the cockchafers struggle in vain to escape by opening the stamens. But it is not until the next day, at nightfall, that the flower, now pink and odorless, releases them. Panic-stricken, the insects flee, passing over the now open stamens and covering themselves in pollen. Forgetting their misadventure, they then launch themselves into other water lilies that will thus pick up the precious pollen they are carrying. Water lilies that grow in temperate zones have a more welcoming attitude to their pollinators, offering them sugary nectar in exchange for carrying their pollen. Water lily flowers only open when the sun is expected to shine because it is on fine days that insects abound. Once fertilized, the plant produces a fruit that ripens, drops off, and falls to the bottom of the water. As this breaks up, it releases seeds which, surrounded by a small cushion of air, rise to the surface and, drifting with the wind, float away from the mother plant. Little by little, the envelope of air bubbles begins to disseminate and the seeds once again sink to the bottom of the water, where they germinate. The seed then puts out a new stem on which leaves and flowers will develop, and the plant's reproductive cycle will begin once more.

[1] Purple Pitcher Plant (*Sarracenia purpurea*). Despite its carnivorous nature, its flowers are fertilized by insects. [2] Water Hawthorn (*Aponogeton distachyos*). [3] and [6] Sacred Lotus (*Nelumbo nucifera*). [4] and [5] Round-leaved Sundew (*Drosera rotundifolia*). This plant grows in damp peat bogs where it captures small insects.

[left] The Water Hyacinth (*Eichhornia crassipes*) is an invasive plant that has colonized most still water areas in tropical countries.
[1] Marsh Marigold (*Caltha palustris*). Its dried leaves can be used as a tobacco substitute to help quit smoking.
[2] Mexican Butterwort (*Pinguicula moranensis*).
[3] Iris (*Iris hookeriana*).
[4] The Yellow Flag Iris (*Iris pseudacorus*) has been the emblem of the kings of France since the time of Clovis.

[1] Marsh Thistle (*Cirsium palustre*).
[2] Mexican Water Lily (*Nymphaea mexicana*).
[3] Duck Potato (*Sagittaria latifolia*). The shape of its leaves has also earned it the name "Broad Leaf Arrowhead."
[4] The Yellow Pond Lily (*Nuphar luteum*) is a common sight in areas of still water.
[5] Yellow Loosestrife (*Lysimachia vulgaris*).
[6] Water Lily 'Arc-en-Ciel' (*Nymphaea* hybrid).
[7] Golden Club (*Orontium aquaticum*). Its dried seeds are edible.

423

[1] Water Lily 'James Hudson'
(*Nymphaea* hybrid).
[2] Grass of Parnassus (*Parnassia palustris*).
Its seeds are so minute that 300,000 of them
weigh only 1/5 oz. (1 gram).
[3] Water Lily 'Jack Wood' (*Nymphaea* hybrid).
[4] Giant Water Lily (*Victoria regia*). Its giant
leaves can support the weight of a child.

[5] Water Lily 'Hollandia' (*Nymphaea* hybrid).
[6] Marsh Cinquefoil (*Comarum palustre*). This species can grow at an altitude of over 6,500 ft. (2,000 m) in wet ground.
[7] Knotweed (*Persicaria bistorta*).
[8] Water Lily 'Meteor' (*Nymphaea* hybrid).

There is almost no place on earth that plants have not managed to conquer: from the frozen poles to the most arid deserts, to city centers where even on asphalt, certain species, though constantly trodden underfoot, manage to survive and bloom.

The closer they are to the poles, the harder it becomes for plants to find the conditions they need to develop and grow. At the poles the temperature remains constantly below freezing; blizzards prevail and the seasons are limited to one very short summer period and a winter spent in almost total darkness.

The first plants to venture into this hostile territory were the campions, catchflies (silenes), and rock jasmines (androsaces) which, in order to survive, had to grow, flower, and set seed in under two months. Though entirely different from this almost lifeless environment, towns and cities in their own way also represent a particularly harsh environment for plants. Nevertheless, with complete disregard for pollution, some plants spring up on roads, sidewalks, and walls. In the most unexpected places, a careful observer will discover an astonishingly diversified range of flora. Wallflowers are often found on church buildings. Wedged into crevices in old stones they rise up, straining towards the bellowers and gargoyles. A little lower down, their neighbors include red valerian and celandines. Some "masochistic" species seem only to take up residence on busy, crowded pathways. In fact, the rounded chamomile grows

Survivor Plants

directly on tarmac; the coltsfoot sets up home on embankments; the butterfly bush (buddleia) colonizes building sites and wasteland, often sharing its territory with the tree of heaven; and the Canada fleabane enjoys growing in cracks in paving, its roots often pushing up the slabs. Knotgrass and bittersweet prefer gutters where they can find humidity and food...quite undaunted by the pollutants pouring into them.

[1] Yellow Alpine Poppy (*Papaver rhaeticum*).
[2] Greater Celandine (*Chelidonium majus*) growing in the trunk of a hollow tree.
[3] *Epidendrum spicatum*. This epiphytic orchid is endemic in the Galapagos Islands.
[4] Spring Gentian (*Gentiana verna*).
[5] The Yellow Wallflower (*Erysimum cheiri*) is at home on churches and monasteries.
[6] The Goldmoss Stonecrop (*Sedum acre*) grows on walls and roofs.

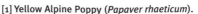

[1] Rock Samphire (*Crithmum maritimum*).
[2] Bamboo (*Phyllostachys* sp.). It is extremely unusual for bamboo to flower and after flowering the plant dies.
[3] Spanish Angelica (*Angelica heterocarpa*).

[4] Large-flowered Houseleek (*Sempervivum grandiflorum*).
[5] Greater Celandine (*Chelidonium majus*).
[6] Knotgrass or Birdweed (*Polygonum aviculare*) even grows on asphalt.
[7] Crusted Saxifrage (*Saxifraga cristata*).

Survivor Plants

5 6

7

[1] Canadian Fleabane (*Erigeron canadensis*).
[2] Buddleia (*Buddleja davidii*) has even made itself at home in the Place de la Concorde in Paris.
[3] The Morettiana Campanula (*Campanula morettiana*) grows among rocks.
[far right] Sempervivum (*Sempervivum funckii*).

[1] Saxifrage (*Saxifraga cotyledon*).
[2] Houseleek (*Sempervivum tectorum*).
[3] Sea Thrift (*Armeria maritima*) grows directly on the limestone rocks of the Burren Plateau in Ireland.
[4] Cobweb Houseleek (*Sempervivum arachnoideum*).
[5] Pineapple Weed (*Matricaria discoidea*) grows on footpaths.
[6] Spiny Spurge (*Euphorbia spinosa*).

P
lants that tolerate salty conditions are very useful along the coast as they help to stabilize sand dunes. They also encourage the creation of new growing environments by trapping alluvium in their roots.

With their feet in the sand and regularly covered in salt water, salicornias (glassworts) grow on beaches right along the Atlantic and Mediterranean shores. These strange halophiles (salt-loving plants) appear to have no leaves or flowers.

Seashore Plants

However, on closer inspection, their stems are seen to be covered in tiny teeth or bristles, which are their leaves, and in minute loculi that conceal tiny green flowers. Salicornias are among the plants most able to tolerate high concentrations of salt in the water and in the soil. Their stems, which crunch like broken glass when trodden underfoot, absorb humidity from the sea air. The sea carries their seeds, the salt gradually dissolving the surrounding seed envelope, and they are then able to germinate in the moist sand.

Salicornias are edible and have medicinal properties. Their stems are eaten like asparagus, their bitter, salty taste acting as a reminder of their habitat. In the past, sailors used to take them on long voyages as they were believed to protect against scurvy.

Other plants that grow on beaches in full sunlight and are exposed to salt spray include the sea bindweed, the sea campion, and the beach grasses. In tropical countries, mangroves have colonized the salty shorelines of warm seas, creating mangrove swamps. Their stilt-like roots trap alluvium, providing a home for a large number of animal species. Little by little, mangrove swamps turn into fertile land on which other plants become established and eventually drive out the mangroves themselves.

[1] The Tree Echium (*Echium* sp.) grows on the shores of the Canary Islands.

[2] and [3] Sea Holly (*Eryngium maritimum*).

[4] Sea Lavender (*Limonium vulgare*). Its flowers are excellent in dried flower arrangements.

[5] Sea Campion (*Silene maritima*).

[6] Cotton Lavender (*Santolina chamaecyparissus*).

[7] Silver Sea Stock (*Malcolmia littorea*).

[1] Goat's Foot (*Ipomoea pes-caprae*). On the island of Réunion, people bathe in a decoction of this plant to get rid of bad luck.
[2] Canary Samphire (*Crithmum latifolium*).
[3] Sand Bedstraw (*Galium arenarium*).
[4] Fetid Passionflower (*Passiflora foetida*).
[5] Yellow-horned Poppy (*Glaucium luteum*). If ingested, this plant can cause delirium and damage the nerve cells of the brain.
[6] Thyme-leaved Toadflax (*Linaria thymifolia*).

[left] Stock (*Matthiola incana*) is commonly found on the coastal sand dunes of the Landes region of south-west France.
[1] Lotus allionii.
[2] Rough Cocklebur (*Xanthium strumarium*).
[3] Giant Fennel (*Ferula communis*). Its stems were once used to punish naughty schoolchildren.
[4] Sea Grape (*Coccoloba uvifera*). Its fermented fruit produces a kind of sparkling wine.

[1] Sea Daffodil (*Pancratium maritimum*). Its poisonous bulbs affect the nervous system.
[2] Sea Stork's Bill (*Erodium maritimum*).
[3] Curry Plant (*Helichrysum stoechas*). So-called because its flowers smell of curry.
[4] Sweet Alyssum (*Alyssum maritimum*).
[5] Sea Bindweed (*Convolvulus soldanella*).
[6] Golden Samphire (*Inula crithmoides*).

448

4

5

6

Index

Common and botanical names of the plants shown in the photographs

All the photographs in this book were taken by Michel Viard/Horizon Features

Other titles in the 1001 photos collection

[1001 photographs]

[1001 photographs]

Flowers
[1001]
[photos]

[1001] photos
Flowers

© 2007 Copyright SA, France
© 2008 Rebo International b.v., Lisse, Netherlands

Text and photo: Michel Viard
Editoral coordination: Gracieuse Licari
Photographic design: Peggy Huynh Quan-Suu
Graphic design: Gwénael Le Cossec
Typesetting: A. R. Garamond, Prague, Czech Republic
Translated by Alayne Pullen in association with First Edition Translations Ltd.,
Cambridge, UK
Edited by First Edition Translations Ltd.,
Cambridge, UK
Copy editor: Jeffrey Rubinoff, Erin Ferretti Slattery

ISBN 978 90 366 2413 8